D1060050

The Cato Institute

The Cato Institute is named for the libertarian pamphlets *Cato's Letters,* which were inspired by the Roman Stoic Cato the Younger. Written by John Trenchard and Thomas Gordon, *Cato's Letters* were widely read in the American colonies in the early eighteenth century and played a major role in laying the philosophical foundation for the revolution that followed.

The erosion of civil and economic liberties in the modern world has occurred in concert with a widening array of social problems. These disturbing developments have resulted from a major failure to examine social problems in terms of the fundamental principles of human dignity, economic welfare, and justice.

The Cato Institute aims to broaden public policy debate by sponsoring programs designed to assist both the scholar and the concerned layperson in analyzing questions of political economy.

The programs of the Cato Institute include the sponsorship and publication of basic research in social philosophy and public policy; publication of major journals on the scholarship of liberty and commentary on political affairs; production of debate forums for radio; and organization of an extensive program of symposia, seminars, and conferences.

CATO INSTITUTE
747 Front Street
San Francisco, California 94111

Is Government the Source of Monopoly?
and Other Essays

Is Government the Source of Monopoly? and Other Essays

Yale Brozen

With a Foreword by David R. Henderson

CATO PAPER No. 9

INSTITUTE
San Francisco, California

"Is Government the Source of Monopoly?" is reprinted with permission from *The Intercollegiate Review,* Winter 1968/69.

"The Attack on Concentration" is reprinted with permission from the *Clemson University Review of Industrial Management and Textile Science*, Vol. 18, No. 1, Spring 1979.

Library of Congress Cataloging in Publication Data

Brozen, Yale, 1917–
    Is Government the source of monopoly? and other essays.

    (Cato paper ; no. 9)
    Bibliography: p.
    CONTENTS: Is Government the source of monopoly?—Are U. S. manufacturing markets monopolized?—The attack on concentration.
        1. Industry and state—United States. 2. Monopolies—United States. 3. Industrial concentration—United States.
    I. Title.
    HD3616.U47B7   338.8'2'0973   80-14176
    ISBN 0-932790-09-7

Printed in the United States of America.

CATO INSTITUTE
747 Front Street
San Francisco, California 94111

CONTENTS

Foreword   *David R. Henderson*   ix

Is Government the Source of Monopoly?   1

Are U.S. Manufacturing Markets Monopolized?   23

The Attack on Concentration   43

Recommended Reading   55

About the Author   59

FOREWORD

"People of the same trade seldom meet together, even for merriment and diversion, but the conversation ends in a conspiracy against the public, or in some contrivance to raise prices. It is impossible indeed to prevent such meetings, by any law which either could be executed, or would be consistent with liberty and justice. But though the law cannot hinder people of the same trade from sometimes assembling together, it ought to do nothing to facilitate such assemblies; much less to render them necessary."[1]

A few years ago a friend of mine and one of his colleagues, both economics professors, were discussing monopoly. My friend's colleague made light of the idea that government regulation is the main source of monopoly, and my friend started to reel off examples, the first of which was trucking regulation. When he pointed out that people are required by law to get a license to operate a common carrier truck and that their applications are often refused, his colleague was stunned. "You mean that if I want to, I can't just go out and operate a truck and offer my services to anyone who wants them?" he asked incredulously. "Why that's ridiculous. How can that possibly be justified? There can't be such a law."

There is such a law. Why didn't this economist know about it? Like many of us, he had received his economics training during the late sixties and early seventies when a monopolistic industry was usually defined in industrial organization economics classes as one in which four firms sell more than a certain percent (usually 50 to 80 percent) of the industry's output, whether or not entry into the industry is restricted. In the last few years the emphasis has changed. Professors in graduate economics courses now emphasize that government itself is a source of monopoly, pointing out that such measures as licensing requirements restrict supply and raise prices.

[1]Adam Smith, *The Wealth of Nations* (New York: The Modern Library, 1937) p. 128.

More important, when economists want to demonstrate that prices are higher under monopoly than they would be under competition, they generally use as evidence monopolies created by government. This evidence is reasonably clear-cut and noncontroversial because the prices before and after monopolization can be compared. When economists attempt to give examples of monopoly not enforced by government, however, they can rarely agree on examples. They agree that the trucking industry is a monopoly, but do not agree about the computer industry. Even economists who believe that concentrated industries are monopolistic do not think that these industries sell at a price much above their cost. For instance, the Federal Trade Commission's Bureau of Economics found that in a sample of 100 concentrated industries where monopoly was claimed to exist, prices exceeded costs by an average of only 3.16 percent. And they got this result with assumptions that would tend to bias this number upward![2] Compare this small excess of prices over cost with the usual estimates that Interstate Commerce Commission (ICC) regulation raises rates between 20 and 40 percent[3] or with the fact that average air fares fell by 10 percent between October 1977 and July 1978, a period of de facto deregulation by the Civil Aeronautics Board (CAB).[4] During this same period, prices in general and fuel prices in particular were rising. Even intermediate microeconomics textbooks are putting more emphasis on government as a creator of monopolies.[5]

Yale Brozen deserves much of the credit for this shift. His research in economic concentration and industry profitability casts doubt on the idea that concentrated industries are monopolistic, and he has drawn together much research on government as a source of monopoly, making it accessible to a wider audience.

[2]Memorandum from Bureau of Economics and Office of Policy Planning and Evaluation to Federal Trade commission (March 30, 1972), quoted in Wesley J. Liebeler, "Market Power and Competitive Superiority in Concentrated Industries," *UCLA Law Review* 25 (1978): 1268.

[3]Thomas Gale Moore, *Freight Transportation Regulation* (American Enterprise Institute for Public Policy Research, Washington, D.C., Nov. 1972).

[4]Conversation with Mark Kahan, Assistant Director of Fares, Rates, and Tariffs, Civil Aeronautics Board, February 14, 1980.

[5]See for example, Jack Hirshleifer, *Price Theory and Applications* (Englewood Cliffs, N.J.: Prentice Hall Inc., 1976) and Edwin Mansfield, *Microeconomics: Theory and Applications,* 3rd ed. (New York: W. W. Norton and Company, 1979).

In the first two essays reprinted here, Professor Brozen gives evidence that monopoly tends to exist only where it is enforced. In the first essay, "Is Government the Source of Monopoly?" he points to many government-created cartels: the trucking cartel, the airline cartel, the ocean freight cartel, and the taxicab cartel. In the second essay, "Are U.S. Manufacturing Markets Monopolized?" he argues that high accounting returns on net worth tend to drop and low accounting returns tend to rise over time, which is consistent with the idea that resources migrate from low-return to high-return industries, making monopoly only temporary. He notes that severe empirical problems arise when accounting rates of return are used to measure real economic profit rates. One problem that is especially relevant during a period of inflation is that economists do not revalue assets upward to reflect increased replacement costs, making older firms appear to have higher profit rates than new firms. In the third essay, he argues that antitrust laws have often hindered competition by preventing large, efficient firms from expanding production. The result, he points out, is that prices are higher and output is lower in these industries, precisely the opposite of the result most economists expect and want from antitrust laws.

Why do monopolies in unregulated markets tend to erode while permanent monopoly generally exists only when enforced by government? The wording of the question almost gives the answer. Government can *enforce* monopoly: It can use its coercive power to fine a firm that cuts prices below government-regulated levels or to fine a new firm that tries to compete in an industry. If the firm's owners persist, they can ultimately be imprisoned. Private firms, on the other hand, have no power to enforce monopoly. They may conspire to fix prices, but each party to such an agreement can almost always gain more by cheating and pricing below the agreed level. For this reason, most collusive agreements are short-lived. (Of course, consistent advocates of freedom to contract must question whether it is sufficient to depend on cheating for protection against monopoly since, presumably, the cartel members could write a collusive contract that the courts would have to enforce. Even if collusive agreements were enforced in a free society, however, a firm outside the agreement, drawn to the industry by the prospect of high profits, would not be bound by such a contract as it is now bound to government-enforced laws that monopolize. New entrants weaken a cartel by expanding market output and the driving the price below the cartel price. The prospect of new supplies entering the market, almost as much as cheating, has been the bane of many cartels.)

Professor Brozen points out that when Adam Smith wrote *The Wealth of Nations* it was clear to everyone that monopolies were the result of government power and that the word "monopoly" was used to mean a special privilege granted by the monarch—the privilege of being the sole supplier of a commodity or service. The lesson of the eighteenth century applies just as much to the twentieth century, as Brozen's first essay amply documents. That the government could virtually end monopoly simply by refraining from granting it makes one wonder why antitrust laws are justified at all, especially since they have, as Brozen points out, often worsened the problem they were designed to solve. It is disappointing, therefore, that Brozen does not challenge the idea of antitrust. Although he does not explicitly advocate antitrust, he cites the dissolutions of Standard Oil and American Tobacco in 1911 as examples of appropriate use of antitrust. Recent research, however, calls into question whether even these dissolutions, previously thought of as obviously successful, were effective. Professor Malcolm Burns of the University of Kansas found that dissolution did not significantly reduce these firms' stock prices and concluded that either the breakups did not reduce their monopoly power or the firms were not monopolies in the first place.[6] Either way, his findings do not support antitrust.

I know many economists who are generally strong free-market advocates but who still call for antitrust on the basis of little evidence. In fact, a prominent free-market economist once told me that he advocates antitrust, not because he himself believes in it, but because many other economists would not take him seriously if he rejected it. Twenty years ago few economists would have advocated eliminating the CAB or the ICC. They began to consider such a step only after some of their colleagues who did research on those agencies called for their abolition. By 1974, however, twenty-one of the twenty-three economists who attended President Ford's economic summit, economists with widely differing beliefs, felt comfortable enough to sign a statement calling for

[6]Malcolm R. Burns, "The Competitive Effects of Trust-Busting: A Portfolio Analysis," *Journal of Political Economy* 85, no. 4 (August 1977): 717-39.

ending the CAB and ICC restrictions on entry and rates. This would not have happened, and we would not be as close as we are to getting rid of those agencies, if the first few economists had withheld their call for abolition for fear of their colleagues' derision.

The same lesson applies to antitrust laws. Economists who have criticized government regulations that create monopoly and antitrust laws allegedly designed to prevent monopoly, and who hesitate to call for ending antitrust laws on the grounds that it sounds radical, could take a lesson from the socialists, who are not bothered by the prospect of sounding too radical. Professor Friedrich Hayek pointed out that "socialist thought owes its appeal to the young largely to its visionary character."[7] He went on to say:

> The main lesson which the true liberal must learn from the success of the socialists is that it was their courage to be Utopian which gained them the support of the intellectuals and thereby an influence on public opinion which is daily making possible what only recently seemed utterly remote. Those who have concerned themselves exclusively with what seemed practicable in the existing state of opinion have constantly found that even this has rapidly become politically impossible as the result of changes in a public opinion which they have done nothing to guide.[8]

When I was eighteen years old and first read Yale Brozen's essay, "Is Government the source of Monopoly?" it gave me much intellectual ammunition for my arguments for a free society. I never dreamed when I read it that I would be writing a foreword to a reprint of it. Maybe someday he will write an article, "Let's Abolish Antitrust Laws," and an eighteen year old will read it and later write a foreword to it. And maybe by then the idea will not seem so radical because we will have learned that the threat to our wealth and our freedom comes not from the freely-acquired control over resources by successful firms but from the coercively-obtained power over resources exercised by government.

February 1980   David R. Henderson
                                                   Senior Policy Analyst
                                                   Cato Institute

---

[7]Friedrich Hayek, "The Intellectuals and Socialism," *University of Chicago Law Review, Economics* (Chicago: University of Chicago Press, 1967).
[8]Ibid.

Is Government the Source
of Monopoly?

When Adam Smith wrote *The Wealth of Nations,* there was no doubt in the mind of anyone that monopolies were the result of government power. Few felt they could flourish without state support. The only prominent monopolies were the result of government grants, and even they were difficult to maintain despite the use of government power. Competition kept breaking out in spite of official attempts to suppress it. The following account is illustrative.

In 1631 the King granted to a group of projectors the exclusive right to make soap of vegetable oil for fourteen years. They agreed to pay the King £4 a ton and to make five thousand tons a year at 3d. a pound; they were permitted, in view of the supposed superiority of their soap, to examine all other manufactured soap and impound or destroy any that they thought below standard. At a test held in private in London, their soap was certified better than that of the London soap-makers. It did not fare so well at Bristol where a tavern maid and a laundress lathered away in public at some soiled linen napkins with the projectors' soap and with soap made by the Bristol soap-makers; they demonstrated that the Bristol soap washed whiter and more economically than the projectors' soap. In spite of this the King ordered the closing down of seven out of Bristol's eleven soap-boiling workshops.

In London the struggle went on with unabated venom. The King's projectors prevailed on the King to prohibit the use of fish oil in soap altogether; on the strength of this they seized the stock of the London soap-makers and prosecuted them in the Star Chamber, following this up by an offer to buy them out of business. The London soap-makers refused the bait and some of them were imprisoned. Murmurs were now rising on all sides. While fishing companies were affected by the prohibition on whale oil, the people in general declared that the projectors' soap was bad. The projectors mobilized the Queen's ladies to write testimonials to the excellence of their soap but laundresses and—more important—cloth-workers throughout the country continued to condemn it. In response the King prohibited the private making of soap altogether and gave the projectors the right to enter and search any private house. All in vain. By the summer of 1634 illicit soap was being sold at a shilling the pound or six times its original price, so low was the general opinion of the projectors' soap. At this point the projectors gave up their plan of using only vegetable oil and took to using the fish oil, which they had made illegal for everyone else. In a final effort to drive their rivals out of business the King put a tax of £4 a ton on Bristol soap. The Bristol soap-boilers refused to pay, and fourteen of them followed the London soap-makers to prison. The farce could not continue much longer and in 1637 the King wound up the project and bought in the projectors' rights for £40,000, of which he made the London soap-makers contribute half. He then allowed the London men to go back to their interrupted manufacture on payment of a tax of £8 a ton to the Crown.[1]

The very word monopoly was, in its usage in the eighteenth century, a label for a special privilege granted by the monarch—the privilege of being the sole supplier of some commodity or service. The royal grant of a monopoly was usually made to a subject of the monarch who, for some reason, the monarch felt deserved enrichment, and it was cheaper to the monarch to award such a privilege than to make a direct grant from the royal purse.

In some cases the excuse for the grant was the encouragement of a trade—as in the case of the grant to the East India Company (famous in American history for the fate of one of its tea cargoes in Boston Harbor in the early 1770s).

As is clear from American history, one of the causes of the American Revolution was the attempt to enforce the Trade and Navigation Acts. These laws were intended to monopolize certain activities for the benefit of Englishmen living in the British Isles. One might say that the American Revolution and the Declaration of Independence were a reaction to the attempt by the British government to create a monopoly by its trade regulation.

Adam Smith wrote his book in part to demonstrate that a nation will fail to enrich itself if it fosters monopoly. The wealth of a nation grows more rapidly by avoiding monopoly. This was heresy in Adam Smith's day but is now a part of accepted doctrine and embodied in our statutes in the form of the Sherman Act, the Clayton Act, and dozens of state antitrust statutes.

---

[1]The quotation is from Cicely Veronica Wedgwood, *The Great Rebellion,* vol. 1, *The King's Peace, 1637–1641* (London: Collins, 1955). Dame Wedgwood has given permission to reproduce the passage.

With such statutes on the law books and with a government born out of reaction to regulations that fostered monopolies, why is a discussion of monopoly necessary? Certainly government support of monopoly privileges must be an archaic practice of interest only to antiquarians. We certainly cannot have revived the very practices that led us to overthrow a previous government and to establish a new one. The sad truth, notwithstanding our history, is that we have not only reinstituted the very practices against which we once revolted, we have instituted new ones with a much wider reach than those of the British government in the eighteenth century.

Monopolies Directly Created by Government

In 1965, Congress passed a Sugar Act. The act is designed to monopolize the trade in sugar for favored growers of cane in Florida and Louisiana, favored growers of sugar beets mostly located in the Western states, and certain favored foreign suppliers who are allotted a share of the American market. American consumers are to be granted the dubious privilege of being protected from the politically impure supply of sugar that some are willing to sell to them at two cents per pound in order that they may be sure of obtaining politically pure sugar at seven cents a pound. When the constituents of the sugar senators ask, "What have you done for me lately?," the senators will be able to tell them.

The Sugar Act is only one of many such acts. The regulations of government that foster monopoly in both domestic production and foreign production are legion. We have a coffee agreement with several foreign governments allotting them a monopoly of the American coffee market. The Department of Agriculture regulates the production of tobacco, and many other commodities, on a basis that monopolizes the privilege of growing tobacco for those who have land with a history of growing tobacco—a history officially acknowledged by the issuance of an appropriate certificate.

This confinement to a designated few of the right to be in a given economic activity is, of course, the essence of monopoly— that is, the prevention of free entry into a line of business or an occupation. If you or I want to get into the business of growing tobacco or supplying electricity, it is not enough to rent land capable of growing tobacco or to buy a generator and let potential customers know that we are ready to supply them. We have to have the government's permission—and I assure you that you cannot get such permission. The only way you can get into these businesses is by buying out one of the monopolists who is already in the business. The privilege of supplying such commodities and services is reserved for them (or their heirs or assigns).

These few examples of government actions that foster monopoly are illustrative of numerous regulatory activities quite consciously aimed at reserving to favored persons the privilege of supplying goods and services—quite consciously aimed at fostering monopoly and restricting to the favored few the right to engage in certain businesses. I will return to an analysis of the economic consequences of this type of regulation later when I will deal in detail with transportation regulation, the monopoly it fosters, and the losses in national welfare it causes.

Monopolies Indirectly Created by Government

For the moment, let us turn away from regulations deliberately aimed at creating monopolies where none would otherwise exist, and let us consider the kind of regulation that is aimed at other purposes but has the net effect of creating more monopoly, more restrictions on entry into various businesses. Such regulations force labor and capital into inferior, alternative uses where they cannot contribute as much to our national and individual welfare as they could and would if allowed the freedom to enter areas of economic activity now barred to them. These restrictions on the freedom of laborers and capitalists to enter some types of activity hurt them as well as the national economy, causing many to fall into the group labeled as poverty stricken and creating a greater poverty problem.

An example of government regulation that indirectly fosters monopoly is minimum wage legislation—the federal statutes known as the Fair Labor Standards Act, the Davis-Bacon Act, and the Walsh-Healy Act, and the many state statutes setting minimum wage rates for various occupations not covered by the federal statutes. Presumably, the aim of these statutes is the prevention of exploitation of employees by employers. However, the result of these statutes has been to provide a monopoly of some businesses for those firms located nearer to major markets or having a more highly skilled set of employees available to them. Crabmeat packing plants located closer to Washington, Baltimore, Philadelphia, and New York, for example, no longer need be concerned with the competition of North Carolina crabmeat packers. When the minimum wage went to $1.25 on September 3, 1965, North Carolina crab packing plants shut down, causing 1,800 women to lose their jobs and eliminating an outlet for the hundreds of crab fishermen who supplied these plants. These North Carolina plants could not pay $1.25 an hour and the transportation costs required to ship their product to their major markets. The crabmeat packing plants that have lower transportation costs because they are located closer to major markets now have a monopoly of those markets. They need not concern themselves with their former competitors located on remote portions of the North Carolina shore.

The fact that minimum wage legislation results in a monopoly of some kinds of business for those in favorable locations is well recognized by some groups. The New England textile manufacturers have always supported increases in the minimum wage rate. They know that any increase knocks out some of the competition from Southern textile producers and gives New England fabricators a more monopolistic position.

The increase in the minimum wage by federal statute from 40 cents to 75 cents an hour in 1950 played an important role in knocking out 10 percent of the individually owned textile plants (between 1947 and 1954) and 25 percent of those owned by partnerships. Textile plants owned by corporations increased by 5 percent in this period, mainly because of the large number of noncorporate plants driven out of business by the higher minimum wage rate.[2]

The increase in the minimum wage rate from 75 cents to $1 an hour in 1956 also served to reduce the number of textile plants in

---

[2]David E. Kaun, "Minimum Wages, Factor Substitution and the Marginal Producer," *Quarterly Journal of Economics* 79 (August 1965): 478–86.

operation, leaving the remaining firms with fewer competitors and a more monopolistic position.

The cigar and cigarette industry and the leather industry had even more competition knocked out by the federal minimum wage law amendments of 1950 and 1956 than did the textile industry. Fifty percent of individually owned tobacco manufacturing establishments and 60 percent of partnership-owned plants went out of business because of the 1950 minimum wage increase. Another 35 percent disappeared in each category after the enactment of the 1956 minimum wage increase. In the leather goods industry, 10 percent of individually owned factories and one-third of partnership-owned factories disappeared after the enactment of the 1950 increase. The 1956 increase knocked out 3 percent of the remaining individually owned leather product factories and 25 percent of the partnership-owned factories.

Incidentally, these decreases in the number of individually owned establishments that I have described are not the result of a general trend in manufacturing. In all other manufacturing, the number of individually owned factories increased by 17 percent in the period in which the 1950 minimum wage increase was applied and by 8 percent in the period in which the 1956 increase was applied. These other industries use more highly skilled labor whose pay rate was not affected by the minimum wage law, and most of their plants have market-oriented locations.

Here, then, is an instance of monopoly fostered by a government regulation not intended for that specific purpose, but which had that effect.

Other government regulations have a similar, largely unintended effect in promoting monopoly. The recent amendments to the Food and Drug Act have reduced competition in the drug industry. Clearance procedures for new drugs have been made so costly that no company will embark on the research program to develop a new drug unless the drug can be expected to have a sales volume of at least $500,000 per year. Under the old law, investors were willing to put capital into a research program if a drug could be developed that might be expected to have a sales volume of $100,000 per year. The number of new drugs becoming available to compete with old drugs has been greatly reduced by the new law. Incidentally, one of the consequences of the new law was an increase in the profitability of the drug industry.

The Transportation Monopolies Created by Government

Perhaps the most thoroughly regulated activity in our economy is transportation. It is, I would argue, more completely regulated than agriculture or even the narcotics industry. First, let us describe some of the regulatory activities in transportation in terms of the monopoly aspect of the regulations; we can then discuss some of the consequences.

The Interstate Commerce Commission (ICC) limits the number of firms allowed to engage in common carrier transportation. In addition, it actually sets minimum rates below which transportation companies are not allowed to sell. It maintains a price umbrella for truckers, barge lines, coastal steamship operators, and railroads.[3]

The Civil Aeronautics Board (CAB) has set minimum air cargo rates and passenger rates. It has even attempted to regulate the service provided at these rates to prevent one airline from offering a more comfortable seat or more legroom at a given price than another.[4]

The Federal Maritime Board forces steamship lines into the ocean conferences—the privately operated cartels that regulate ocean freight rates and attempt to prevent rate cutting.[5] Forty states regulate intrastate trucking and prevent rate cutting just as the ICC prevents rate cutting in the interstate movement of freight.[6] Most cities regulate the taxi business, with the same result.[7]

The regulatory agencies not only prevent those in the transportation industry from competing with each other—they also protect those in the industry from the entry of additional competi-

---

[3]G. W. Hilton, "Barriers to Competitive Ratemaking," *I.C.C. Practitioners Journal* 29 (June 1962): 1083–96; C. D. Stone, "ICC: Some Reminiscences on the Future of American Transportation," *New Individualist Review* 2 (Spring 1963): 3–15.

[4]S. Peltzman, "CAB: Freedom from Competition," *New Individualist Review* 2 (Spring 1963): 16–24.

[5]John S. McGee, "Ocean Freight Rate Conferences and the American Merchant Marine," *The University of Chicago Law Review* 27 (Winter 1960): 191–314.

[6]Donald Harper, *Economic Regulation of the Motor Trucking Industry by the States* (Urbana: University of Illinois Press, 1959).

[7]Stephen Sobotka, *The Operation and Regulation of Taxicabs in the City of Chicago* (Evanston, Ill.: Transportation Center, 1958).

tors. You cannot get into the trucking business, the airline business, the bus business, the taxi business, or the pipeline business as you would enter retailing or manufacturing. You must be certified by the CAB if you wish to enter the airline business. The ICC will certify an additional common carrier truck company to operate on a given route only if it can be demonstrated that adequate truck service is not available on the route in question. Washington, D.C., is the only major city in which you can start a taxi business simply by applying for a taxi license and demonstrating that you carry the necessary public liability insurance and have safe equipment and drivers. All other major cities stop any additional taxi operators from entering the business. They even prevent present taxi operators from increasing the size of their fleets. Transportation regulation very effectively protects transportation companies from new competition and produces the exact opposite of the situation that our antimonopoly laws were designed to produce in other industries.

Regulation Causes High Rates

The original *raison d'être* for transportation regulation was the prevention of extortionate rate-setting by railroad monopolies and discriminatory treatment of shippers. Yet, from its very inception, the ICC has caused rates to be higher than they otherwise would be and forced some users of freight services to pay very much higher rates than other shippers had to pay.

Before the ICC began operation, agreements between railroads were made in order to maintain certain rate levels for the shipment of corn, for example, from Chicago to New York. However, the railroads seldom observed their agreements. They constantly undercut the agreed rates with very beneficial results for Midwestern farmers. With the enactment of the Interstate Commerce Act, undercutting of the published corn rates from Chicago to New York ceased.

The Act provided that short haul rates were not to be higher than long haul rates. Since this meant that any reduction in long haul between points joined by competing railroads would have to be accompanied by reductions in short haul rates, railroads ceased trying to compete by setting low long-haul rates. Rates between

Chicago and New York went up and stayed up after 1887, the year when the Interstate Commerce Commission began operation.[8]

Since this may sound like such ancient history that it has little application to present circumstances—although I assure you it does—let me discuss a more recent illustration of the impact of regulation in causing rate increases. Although truck transportation of agricultural commodities is exempted from regulation, the ICC regulated truck rates for semiprocessed agricultural goods before 1952. The courts held, in 1952, that the agricultural exemption applied to semiprocessed items as well as raw commodities. Following the deregulation of these goods, motor carrier rates for fresh dressed poultry fell by 33 percent and for frozen poultry by 36 percent over the next five years.[9]

With the passage of the Transportation Act of 1958, motor carriage of semiprocessed items was placed under regulation again. Rates for transporting these goods promptly rose by 20 percent.

Incidentally, I should point out that in the seventeen years before the ICC came into operation, average railroad rates dropped from $19 per 1,000 ton-miles to $8.50. It seems that competition was working very well indeed in the rail industry from 1870 to 1887. In the seventeen years after the ICC began operating, rail rates dropped from $8.50 per 1,000 ton-miles to $7.80 (see figure 1). If there was a large monopoly profit in railroad prices at the time the ICC began operating, the Commission does not seem to have done much about it. Certainly, the record of decreasing rates after the Commission began regulating the industry is nowhere near as impressive as the record in the period when there was no regulation.

The fall in railroad rates from 1870 to 1898 may be attributed to the generally deflationary circumstances of the times. The general level of prices in the United States fell until the time of the Klondike gold strike in 1898. The important point to recognize is that the ICC did nothing to accelerate the decline in rates which had

---

[8]Paul W. MacAvoy, *The Economic Effects of Regulation: The Trunk-Line Railroad Cartels and the Interstate Commerce Commission before 1900* (Cambridge: MIT Press, 1965).

[9]Department of Agriculture estimates reported in "Problems of the Railroads," Hearings before the Subcommittee on Surface Transportation of the Committee on Interstate and Foreign Commerce (U. S. Senate, 88th Congress, Second Session, 1958), p. 2103.

been taking place before the ICC began operating, that it actually caused an increase in rates which had been competitively determined between points joined by more than one railroad, and that in recent years railroads which wanted to offer lower prices to their customers have been refused permission to reduce rates.

A few examples of this refusal are illustrative of a much larger number of instances. In 1951, the Commission denied railroads permission to institute proposed reductions of rates on scrap iron. In this instance, the Commission was holding an umbrella for the barge lines. The Commission also denied a rail request to reduce petroleum product rates that same year to protect trucker business, although the proposed rates were compensatory and railroads would have made money at these rates. In 1954 railroads filed a proposal to reduce rates on magazines from Philadelphia to Texas points. The ICC refused to allow the rate cut to go into effect. This time it was holding an umbrella for coastal steamship operators. In the same year, the ICC rebuffed a rail request to reduce rates on aluminum articles. In 1955 the Commission refused to allow reductions of rail rates on sugar in order to protect barge operators. In 1961 the ICC denied a request to lower rates on piggyback movements. And so the story goes.

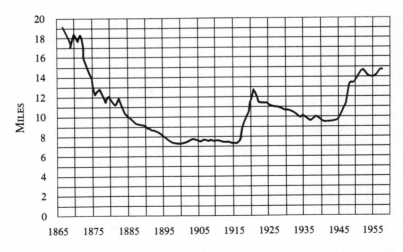

FIGURE 1. Freight Revenue per Ton-Mile of U.S. Railroads, 1867–1958

Regulation Causes Discrimination

This is, to say the least, a weird result of a statute that was presumably designed to limit the ability of railroad monopolies to extract high prices from shippers. Did Congress really intend to force shippers to pay higher prices than they would have to pay in the absence of regulation?

Perhaps Congress did not intend to reduce competition among railroads when it passed the Interstate Commerce Act in 1887, although this was the immediate result. There appears to be no ambiguity on this score since 1920, however. The Transportation Act of 1920 instituted minimum rate regulation of railroads. If it was monopoly about which Congress was concerned, it would hardly have been necessary to place floors under rates. Presumably, the purpose of regulating monopolies is to prevent prices from being high. The usual method and aim in monopoly regulation is to put ceilings on prices at the levels that restrict the monopolist's return on investment to the rate earned in competitive industries of comparable risk and progressiveness. In this conception of the regulatory process, there is no place for minimum rate regulation. The Transportation Act of 1920 frankly converted the ICC into an operator of a cartel, not a regulator of monopolies.[10]

However, the ICC had behaved as a cartel authority long before this time. Presumably, another purpose of the regulation of monopolies is the prevention of monopolistic practices. It is not regarded as equitable for anyone to possess and exercise the power to extract higher prices from some people for the same service that is sold at lower prices to others. Such a practice is regarded by the courts as evidence of the use and exercise of monopoly power and would lead to punitive findings by the courts under the Sherman and Clayton acts.

Yet, under ICC regulation, different rates are set for the transportation of different commodities even when there is no difference in the service or in the cost of providing the service. Before the Interstate Commerce Act was passed, railroads classified

---

[10]Gilbert Burck, "The Great U. S. Freight Cartel," *Fortune* 55 (January 1957): 102; Samuel P. Huntington, "The Marasmus of the ICC: The Commission, the Railroads, and the Public Interest," *Yale Law Journal* 61 (April 1952): 467–509.

freight into four categories on which they attempted to maintain different rates. However, competition among roads in Trunk Line territory caused rate differentiation almost to disappear.[11] After the ICC began operating, rate differentiation proliferated to the point where rates have become a morass of discriminatory charges based on more than 200 classifications. Despite the prohibition of railroad discrimination in the Act to Regulate Commerce of 1887, discrimination increased—with the blessing of the ICC. The rates charged on the movement of some commodities range up to ten times as much on some as on others between the same pair of points for essentially the same service.

The following chart (see figure 2), which simply breaks up rail movement into ten equal classes in terms of the amount of car

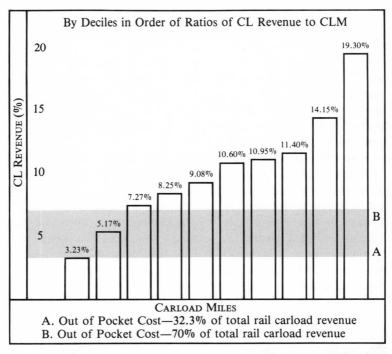

FIGURE 2. Rail Carload Revenue of 261 Commodity Groups Related to Carload Miles, 1960

[11]P. Locklin, *Economics of Transportation,* 6th ed. (Homewood, Ill.: Irwin, 1966).

miles in each class, shows that the 10 percent of car miles charged for at the highest rates pay six times as much per car mile as the 10 percent of car miles charged at the lowest rates.

You will notice that this chart greatly simplifies the rail rate structure to show the gross effects of the discriminatory treatment of shippers. These ten groupings are an amalgam of 261 different commodity groups each charged a different rate with the highest rates being thirty-five times as high as the lowest rates. Some differences in commodity rates are justifiable on the basis of differences in costs. These differences in costs wash out to a large extent, however, when we look at revenue results in dollars-per-carload-mile terms. And we still see a carload mile of some commodities yielding more than ten times as much revenue as a carload mile of other commodities.

By giving the ICC power to set minimum rates, Congress has certainly put us on notice that it is not interested in preventing monopoly or the exercise of monopoly power. If it were, it would give the ICC only the power to set maximum rates. I would also argue that Congress not only wishes to support monopoly and create monopolies where none exist, but it is also in favor of discrimination among shippers. It is not interested in eliminating discrimination despite the proclamation to that effect in the preamble of the Act to Regulate Interstate Commerce.

What Congress is interested in doing is taxing some shippers by seeing that they are charged above-cost rates in order to subsidize other shippers and make freight service available to them at below-cost rates. This has been the intent of Congress and of the regulatory agencies.[12] The net result, however, has been that the shippers that Congress is attempting to favor are paying higher rates than they would be paying if Congress had not attempted to legislate such favors. The situation is reminiscent of the old wisecrack, "With friends like these, who needs enemies?"

Economic legislation in the transportation field produces the opposite of its intended result, just as so much other economic legislation does. The imposition of regulation on the pricing of natural gas in the field, which was intended to produce lower

[12]Robert A. Nelson, "Interest Conflicts in Transportation," *Journal of Business* 37 (April 1964): 167–78; Robert A. Nelson, "Rate-Making in Transportation—Congressional Intent," *Duke Law Journal* 1960: 221–38.

prices for consumers, has caused an increase in the field price of
gas.[13] Our tariff legislation, which presumably protects high-wage
American workers from the competition of low-paid foreigners,
actually monopolizes low-paying jobs and prevents Americans
from moving into higher-paying jobs.[14] Our minimum wage legislation, which is supposed to eliminate poverty by raising the pay
of low-paid workers, is creating more poverty by causing unemployment and by forcing people out of higher-paying jobs into
poorly paid jobs.[15] Our legislation favoring low-income regions
(such as the Tennessee Valley and Appalachia), which is supposed
to benefit the poor, is maintaining pockets of poverty and
benefiting the highly paid workers.[16] Our agricultural program,
presumably designed to help poor farmers, has hurt poor farmers
and enriched rich farmers.[17] Our urban renewal programs, which
are supposed to benefit the slum dweller, have hurt slum dwellers
and small business men and enriched building contractors, land-
lords, and the most highly paid workers in the country, the members of the building trades unions.[18]

The Result of Congressional Intent in Transportation

Despite the congressional intent to tax some shippers through
imposition of high rates in order to subsidize other shippers by
making below-cost rates available, the net result has been that the
shippers who are supposed to be favored are paying higher rates
than they would be paying if Congress had not tried to do them a
favor. Congress has tried to keep common carriers profitable

[13]Robert W. Gerwig, "Natural Gas Production: A Study of Costs of Regulation,"
Journal of Law and Economics 5 (October 1962): 69-92.

[14]Yale Brozen, "The New Competition—International Markets: How Should We
Adapt?" *Journal of Business* 33 (October 1960): 322-26.

[15]Yale Brozen, "Minimum Wage Rates and Household Workers," *Journal of Law
and Economics* 5 (October 1962): 103-9.

[16]Yale Brozen, "The Role of Open Markets in Coordinating and Directing Economic Activity," in *Futures Trading Seminar* (Madison, Wis.: Mimir, 1966).

[17]D. Gale Johnson, "Output and Income Effects of Reducing the Farm Labor
Force," *Journal of Farm Economics* 42 (November 1960): 779-96.

[18]Joel Segall, "The Propagation of Bulldozers: A Review Article," *Journal of
Business* 38 (October 1965): 397-402. This article reviews Martin Anderson, *The
Federal Bulldozer* (Cambridge: MIT Press, 1964).

while extending below-cost rates to small shippers and to shippers of agricultural commodities by giving the ICC the power to set high rates—above-cost rates—for less worthy shippers. In this way, it was hoped, common carriers could earn enough to attract the necessary capital to the transportation business and yet provide below-cost service to the worthy shippers—those with political preference (or, should I say, political clout).

How has it happened, then, that the shippers who are subsidized are worse off than if there had been no attempt to subsidize them? Perhaps the way to explain this is to begin with a paradox. In 1956, after rising labor rates had greatly eroded the return on railroad capital, the ICC raised rail rates by 6 percent. The St. Louis-San Francisco R.R., after putting the new rates into effect, found that its volume of freight movement increased by 2 percent in the following year, but that its total revenues dropped by 1 percent. Now how can you charge higher prices, do more business, and end up with less revenue?

To explain the paradox, let us look at the following set of figures (see figure 3). Suppose a railroad is doing 150 billion ton-

	Freight Rate	Volume	Revenue
CLASS I	1¢/ton–mile	100 bil. ton–miles	$1,000 bil.
CLASS II	6¢/ton–mile	50 bil. ton–miles	3,000 bil.
		150 bil. ton–miles	4,000 bil.
AVERAGE	2.67¢		
10% Increase Across-the-Board			
CLASS I	1.1¢/ton–mile	112 bil. ton–miles	$1,232 bil.
CLASS II	6.6¢/ton–mile	41 bil. ton–miles	2,706 bil.
		153 bil. ton–miles	3,938 bil.
AVERAGE	2.57¢	+ 2%	−1.5%

FIGURE 3. Examples of Increased Freight Rates with Increased Volume and Reduced Revenues

miles of business and realizing $4 billion of revenue with an average revenue of 2.67 cents per ton-mile. This average is the result of doing 100 billion ton-miles at 1 cent per ton-mile, let us say, and 50 billion ton-miles at 6 cents per ton-mile. Some shippers are being charged a high price, but this does not result in a handsome return to the railroad. The profit from the high-price business subsidizes the loss suffered on the business done at a low price.

Now let us assume that the loss becomes so great that prices must be raised if the railroad is to stay in business. For this example, let us assume they are raised 10 percent. This amounts to a 0.1 cent increase on the subsidized business and a 0.6 cent increase on the high-rated business. As a consequence of the increases, the high-rated business falls off. The railroad has a substantial increase in low-rated business and its volume increases by 2 percent, but revenues fall, despite the higher prices charged. The reason lies in the decline in high-rated business which more than offsets the price increase and the rise in volume of low-rated traffic.

High-rated shippers have been leaving the railroads and common carrier truckers in large numbers because the price of service is high and has been increased. They are finding it cheaper to buy their own trucks and barges and to build their own pipelines rather than allow themselves to be grossly overcharged.

We can see the net result of this in terms of the rapid growth of private carriage from 23 percent of total intercity ton-miles in 1948 to 32 percent in 1960. This growth in private carriage came at the expense of the high-rated traffic of the railroads and common carrier trucks. Although the common carrier share of intercity traffic dropped only from 77 to 68 percent of the total between 1948 and 1960, their share of the intercity freight bill which they collected dropped from 74 to 57 percent. Their share of freight revenues dropped by 23 percent while their share of ton-miles dropped by only 12 percent.

Because high-rated traffic is fleeing the railroads, the high-rated business done by railroads declined by one-third during the last fifteen years while total intercity traffic was rising by 50 percent. This reduction in volume means that the rates to preferred shippers have had to be increased because of the decline in the share of the overhead burden carried by the vanishing high-rated traffic. Rates paid by the preferred traffic have now been increased to a level higher than they would have been if there had been no attempt to tax some shippers for the benefit of the preferred traffic.

The ICC, in its attempt to favor low volume shippers, suppressed the railroads' initial attempts to institute multicar and trainload discounts for volume shipments.[19] The result has been that much of this large-volume traffic has now moved to pipelines and barges. Low-volume shippers, as a consequence, are now paying higher rates than they would have if the ICC had allowed some so-called discrimination in favor of large-volume shippers. The supposedly scandalous behavior of the railroads in the nineteenth century in giving rebates to large shippers was simply an attempt to hold traffic that would have been lost without the rebates.

The ICC has now allowed trainload volume discounts on coal since the electric utilities would have built slurry pipelines and high-voltage transmission lines from mine mouth generating plants if this had not been done. If volume rates had been allowed when railroads first requested them, there would be far more traffic on railroads today, less overhead or burden per unit of traffic, and lower current prices to the shippers Congress and the ICC were trying to subsidize.

Who Has Benefited from Regulation

The value-of-service rate-making principle that has been enforced by the ICC is one designed to extort monopoly returns from the carriage of high-value commodities. Since the evidence indicates that low-volume shippers and low-value commodities have not benefited from the monopoly returns extracted from some shippers, who has received these returns? Certainly investors in railroads have not received them! The return on railroad investment has averaged less than 5 percent for at least the past forty-five years. The monopoly profits made on some transportation business appear to have gone almost entirely to members of labor unions, to labor union officers, and to subsidizing the employment of unneeded employees.

[19]Paul W. MacAvoy and James Sloss, *Regulation of Transport Innovation: The ICC and Unit Coal Trains to the East Coast* (New York: Random House, 1967).

In this period in which trucking regulation was instituted and in which strong support was given to the unionization of employees (1929–1947), average earnings of employees in the highway freight and warehousing industry rose by 135 percent. This may be compared with the 86 percent rise in the annual earnings of the average employee in all private industry. I would estimate that by 1947, employees in the regulated trucking industry were being overpaid by at least 10 percent. By 1966, the extent of overpayment had grown to at least 15 percent.

In an industry whose wage bill exceeds $6 billion, this means that overpayment of employees consumes $800 million of the industry's revenues. Since profits in common carrier trucking were on the order of $300 million in 1966, employees of the industry received about three times as much in *overpayment* as investors received as a return on their capital. Certainly not as much as half of the return to trucking companies could conceivably be considered as monopoly profits conferred by the ICC. Using a maximum estimate of the monopoly profits of investors and a minimum estimate of the monopoly profits of unionized employees, employees received five times the amount of monopoly profits as investors in regulated trucking companies. The example of this one mode indicates that if any monopoly returns are being earned in the transportation industry, practically all of it goes to the employees.

In the railroad industry, investors as a whole obtain no monopoly profits. Their capital is earning less than it could have earned in alternative uses. Employees probably receive about $600 million in overpayment for their services, although a major part of this may be regarded as coming at the expense of railroad investors rather than at the expense of shippers. Monopoly profits extracted from some rail shippers by the railroad industry are practically all consumed in providing unneeded services (services worth less than their cost) and in employing unneeded employees. The railroad industry has estimated that it has been paying $500 million per year for unneeded employees (for firemen who do not tend fires, brakemen who do no braking, yard crews who do no yard work, and so on). If the experience of the Florida East Coast Railroad in operating its road since it was struck is any guide, $500 million is a great underestimate of what the railroad industry has been paying for unneeded employees. The figure should be at least double this amount for employees used in freight service alone.

Since federally regulated truckers and railroads do over 90 percent of the business (by dollar volume) done by federally regulated freight carriers, the extraction of monopoly returns to over-compensate trucking employees and to employ unneeded workers in the railroad industry means that most of our common carrier freight services have been overpriced by at least 10 percent. Given value-of-service rate-making, part of the services offered by common carriers has been very greatly overpriced (with the result that some rates came to be called "phantom" rates—rates for traffic that ceased to exist because the rate was so high). These very high rates for some kinds of business drove this kind of business off the common carriers. The growth of private carriage and the decline of common carriage in the past thirty-five years has been a result of this regulatory policy—a policy which operated as if the ICC-regulated portion of the industry were a total monopoly when, at best, it was only a partial monopoly.

The Costs of Regulation

To conclude this analysis, let us sum up the costs imposed on our nation by the cartelization and monopolization of the transportation industry under the aegis of government.

First, as of this writing we are using approximately $1 billion worth of labor services in the railroad industry which are totally wasted. These services could be producing products for us worth $1 billion. Instead, they are producing nothing. These unneeded laborers would not be employed in the rail industry if they could not have been paid for—and they could not have been in the absence of monopolistic prices set on some traffic by the ICC.

Second, we are overpaying employees in trucking, railroading, and airlining at least another billion dollars. If this overpayment were simply a transfer of income from one group to another, we might regard it as inequitable, but not as wasteful or uneconomic. Inasmuch as these overpaid employees are in the upper half of the population in terms of status measured by income, and a major part of their overpayment is at the expense of the poorer half of the population, we may be particularly resentful of such inequity. However, as a professional economist, I have nothing to say on this point.

As an economist, I should point out that the overpayment of employees in transportation causes other results besides a simple transfer of income from the poor to the rich. The $40,000 a year airline pilot and the $20,000 a year milk-truck driver can receive these rates of pay only because many transportation services are overpriced. The overpricing restricts the rate of purchase of these services, prevents resources (manpower and capital) from being used in the most productive way, and causes a loss in net national income because much goes unproduced which would otherwise be turned out. Of the $15 billion of common carriage trucking services purchased each year, about $10 billion would not be purchased if railroads were allowed to reduce their rates on high-rated traffic and innovate special services at premium rates. If this traffic moved by rail, the job could be done with the expenditure of about $3 billion per year of manpower, fuel, and material instead of $10 billion. This would mean a saving of $7 billion a year. It would be possible to add that amount of housing, schooling, medical services, research, recreation, and so on, to our total output of goods and services if we did not waste these resources.

These are the major wastes caused by transportation regulation. We could add various amounts resulting from uneconomic locations chosen to economize on overpriced transportation, uneconomic airline scheduling which results from minimum fare regulation, etc. To the $8 billion of waste described above, these would add approximately $2 billion more.

This is the cost of only one set of monopolies fostered by the government. If we were to add the costs resulting from the cartels in agriculture operated by the Department of Agriculture, the costs of monopolies by license and franchise such as taxi, utility, barber, electrician, plumber, medical, and others, the total cost would come to over $50 billion per year.

I would estimate, then, that our governmentally fostered and supported monopolies cost the country $50 billion per year. In return, we have our freedom to choose our occupation restricted, the value of corrupting civil servants and congressmen increased, and a larger poverty problem on which to work. I, for one, am willing to give up these doubtful values produced by regulation in order to increase our national income by $50 billion or to increase the leisure time available for the pursuit of truth, beauty, and goodness by 15 billion hours.

Are U.S. Manufacturing
Markets Monopolized?

Discussions of monopoly in the United States dwell almost exclusively on the manufacturing industries.*The point of departure of these discussions is primarily bigness and concentration. Typically, a collection of learned inquiries on monopoly such as *Monopoly Power and Economic Performance*[1] includes not one paper dealing with licensure of occupations or limitations on entry into plumbing contracting, liquor and drug retailing, taxi operation, banking, sale of electricity, or truck transportation. Nor do such collections include studies discussing ICC rate floors, sponsorship of cartels by the Department of Agriculture and the Federal Maritime Commission, effects of minimum wage laws on size structure of firms and concentration, limitations on entry and on the introduction of new products imposed by the Food and Drug Administration, or even that generator of monopoly, tariffs. Also, this anthology omits any analysis of the performance of government monopolies such as the Postal Service, the Tennessee Valley Authority, the uranium enrichment service of the Department of Energy, or the numerous local government monopolies of water, electricity, and mass transit.

If one were to believe what is said in the majority of studies analyzing the monopoly problem, any increase in the size of a firm or in concentration must be anticompetitive. The price of rural general-merchandising services, according to them, must have increased as a consequence of the growth of large mail-order organizations, such as Sears Roebuck and Montgomery Ward, concentrating a large share of this business in their hands. Henry Ford is usually lionized for what he did to reduce the price of

---

*From Yale Brozen, *Big Business, Industrial Concentration, and Public Policy,* forthcoming.

[1]E. Mansfield ed., *Monopoly Power and Economic Performance* (New York: W. W. Norton & Company Inc., 1968).

automobiles and raise wages, but the 60 percent share of the market attained by his company in 1921 would be frowned on today as obvious evidence of oligopoly or dominance. The extraordinary returns earned by the Ford Motor Company, frequently exceeding 100 percent, would confirm its antisocial character. That the nearly bankrupt General Motors Company of 1921 would ever surpass Ford or that the then unborn Chrysler Company would outdo Ford by the late 1930s would be inconceivable.[2]

Professor John Galbraith's *The New Industrial State* tells us that a success story like Henry Ford's could never happen in modern America. Today's industrial giants are not as profit-minded as Ford and his ilk, and they do not serve the market as he did. Socialism prevails in the United States. The economy is planned, and that is good. However, it is planned by private organizations—the 500 largest industrial corporations—and that is bad. To improve the situation, "...the educational and scientific estate... [must] become a decisive instrument of political power [under a strongly creative political hand]."[3] The author is not concerned with his "fact" that markets are controlled, but only with who does the controlling. Consumer sovereignty is not one of his values.

Galbraith equates private planning with state planning. He "slips from the proposition that the firm plans to the proposition that the economy is planned without realizing that such statements possess only a verbal similarity."[4] He recognizes no difference between the ability of a private organization to force the market to conform to its plan and the ability of the state, with its powers, to force conformance. Galbraith insists that private organizations, if they are "big in an industry," can influence "prices and costs and command capital [because they have] access to advertising, and selling resources, and possess... the other requisites of market power."[5]

Galbraith tells us that half of all economic activity in the United States goes on in, and is controlled by, the 500 largest in-

[2]W. G. Shepherd, *The Economics of Industrial Organization* (Englewood Cliffs, N.J.: Prentice-Hall Inc. 1979): p. 207.

[3]J. K. Galbraith, *The New Industrial State* (Boston: Houghton Mifflin Company, 1967), p. 294.

[4]S. Gordon, "The Close of the Galbraithian System," *Journal of Political Economy* 76 (1968): 640.

[5]Galbraith, *New Industrial State,* p. 206.

dustrial corporations.[6] His data are not quite accurate. Half of all *manufacturing* employment occurs in the 500. Manufacturing provides only one-fourth of all employment in the United States. This means that the 500 largest industrial corporations provide one-eighth of all employment rather than one-half—a 300 percent error in his assertion.

The problem before us, however, is not to determine how inaccurate Galbraith is, but how to measure monopoly—the ability of a business to control the market rather than be controlled by it. This we must first settle. Then we can move on to a determination of whether the market controls U.S. business or these businesses control the market.

The Structural Test for Monopoly

Galbraith follows a forty-year-old tradition still prevalent among economists. He uses a simple structural test as a measure of market power. He is simpler than almost all economists in using aggregate concentration rather than percentage of a market as his measure of market power. American Motors is among the biggest 500 industrial companies in the United States, ranking in the top quarter of the 500, but its 2 percent share of the domestic market for new automobiles and its 0.6 percent of the domestic market for all automobiles sold in any given year would hardly be regarded as giving it much influence over the price, quantity, or quality of automobiles. A Braeden Aeromotors or a Sanborn Map Company, each "dominant" in its market (windmills and fire insurance maps) but neither qualifying for the list of 500 largest companies, would be said by many economists to have more market power selling 75 to 80 percent of the product offered in their markets than American Motors has with its placement among the 150 largest concerns.

The typical approach among the "bust 'em up" school to the determination of which markets can be said to be monopolized is exemplified by the 1968 report of the antitrust task force headed by Professor Phil Neal. It tells us that an oligopolistic industry is

[6]Ibid. pp. 1–2.

one in which four or fewer firms produce 70 percent or more of that industry's product. It advises that the antitrust laws should be amended to make it possible to break up any oligopolistic firm, that is, any firm that turns out more than 15 percent of its industry's domestic output in an industry where the biggest four do 70 percent or more of the industry's business and the value of the industry's sales exceeds $500 million ($950 million at today's prices).[7]

Economists frequently use the simple structural test employed by the Neal Commission as their method of categorizing markets.[8] However, most do not argue that an oligopolistic market, defined in the manner of the Neal Commission, is necessarily or automatically a cartelized or monopolized market.[9] They readily concede that "seller concentration is a necessary, but not sufficient, condition."[10] They do argue that the cost of explicit collusion is less likely and cartelization (shared monopoly) more likely in concentrated markets.[11]

Analyses of the extent of competition and monopoly in the United States use this same simple structural test in classifying markets.[12] They sometimes include in the monopoly category industries which are not concentrated but in which cartelization is compelled or supported by a government agency. The fluid milk, trucking, and the 1950s air transport markets, for example, fall in this category. Automobiles, photographic equipment, locomotives, chewing gum, corn syrup, biscuits, cigarettes, newsprint,

[7]"Task Force Report on Antitrust Policy," *Trade Regulation Reports,* Supplement to No. 415 (May 26, 1969) at II-13, A-9, A-18 to A-21.

[8]For example, R. Evely and I. M. O. Little, *Concentration in British Industry* (Cambridge: At the University Press, 1960), pp. 8–25.

[9]R. M. Cyert and K. D. George, "Competition, Growth, and Efficiency," *Economic Journal* 79 (1969): 25; George J. Stigler, "Discussion of Report of the Attorney General's Committee on Antitrust Policy," *American Economic Review* 46 (1956): 506.

[10]H. M. Mann, "Seller Concentration, Barriers to Entry, and Rates of Return in Thirty Industries, 1950–1960," *The Review of Economics and Statistics* 48 (August 1966): 296.

[11]G. J. Stigler, "A Theory of Oligopoly," *Journal of Political Economy* 72 (Feb. 1964), reprinted in G. J. Stigler, *The Organization of Industry* (Homewood, Ill.: Richard D. Irwin, 1968).

[12]G. J. Stigler, "Competition in the United States," *Five Lectures On Economic Problems* (London: Longmans, Green, 1949), p. 46. Stigler follows the classification of C. Wilcox, *Competition and Monopoly in American Industry* (1941), which is largely based on concentration ratios.

newspapers, primary aluminum, copper mining are all classed as monopolized in 1939 in a Stigler study primarily on the basis of high concentration ratios.[13]

We may believe the cost of collusion to be low in a highly concentrated industry, suspect that undetected collusion occurs in some of these industries, and even find actual instances of collusion (as in the electrical conspiracy), but it does not follow that all highly concentrated industries should be classed as monopolized or oligopolistic.[14] It can be argued that an industry is not necessarily monopolized even with the actual presence of a scheme for regulating prices and output. Lower output and higher prices may not occur despite a formal agreement among competing firms to privately regulate a market.[15]

A highly concentrated industry may manage to obtain agreement among its members to adhere to assigned quotas and to avoid cutting prices, and yet it may have no influence over its market. If there are no arbitrary barriers to entry and the number of entrepreneurs is abundant,[16] or if customers are large,[17] a cartel will not succeed in controlling the market despite a small number of firms in the industry. The Organization of Petroleum Exporting Countries (OPEC) has enjoyed an unusual success in part because expansion of producing capacity outside OPEC has been hindered by price and allocation controls in the United States and by increasingly onerous tax treatment of oil firms in the United States (especially Alaska), the United Kingdom, Norway, and Indonesia. The Alaskan state government has enacted thirteen tax increases in ten years reducing private returns to investments in North Slope production to 9 percent—less than can be earned by

[13]Stigler adds an industry such as rubber boots and shoes to the Wilcox list of monopoly markets because "the concentration ratio is relatively high." Stigler, *Five Lectures,* p. 58.

[14]"And the systematic disregard of inter-product competition renders almost all of the work with concentration ratios worthless." Ibid., p. 48, note 2. "The availability of substitutes, the size of the market (local, national, and international), the extent of collusion, and other factors will influence the correspondence between concentration and monopoly." Ibid., p. 53. Also see Clair Wilcox, "The Alleged Ubiquity of Oligopoly," *American Economic Review* 40 (May 1950): 67.

[15]A. P. Winston, *Judicial Economics* (Austin, Texas: 1957).

[16]H. Demsetz, "Why Regulate Utilities?" *Journal of Law & Economics* (April 1968): 55–65.

[17]S. H. Lustgarten, "The Impact of Buyer Concentration in Manufacturing Industries," *Review of Economics and Statistics* 57 (1975): 125.

the purchase of U.S. Treasury issues. As a consequence, operators on the North Slope in 1979 abandoned efforts that would
have added a million barrels a day to the U.S. supply.[18] Similarly,
exploration in the North Sea has been cut back because of governmental greed, with the result that annual output planned for the
1980s has fallen by 200 million barrels.

A Dynamic Test for Monopolization

We need better means for determining the presence or absence of
monopoly than simple structural measures. Stigler proposed a test
that is somewhat more useful and indicative than the usual structural tests. If an industry is monopolized, it will tend to earn at
least the average rate of return and, frequently, above average returns on its capital. If monopoly is present, above average rates of
return will frequently *not* tend to move toward the average.[19] This
test is not a sufficient condition for showing the presence of monopoly.[20] The long-run equilibrium position in a competitive
market may move as rapidly as the industry moves toward its
long-run equilibrium position because of recurring unforeseen
positive movements in demand or declines in cost.[21] But if it occurs, it is a condition consistent with the presence of monopoly,
although it is not a proof of the absence of competition.[22]

The test is difficult to apply because the readily available data
are not adequate. The accounting rates of return on equity in various industries compiled by the Internal Revenue Service, the
Securities Exchange Commission, the Federal Trade Commission,
and the First National City Bank are not economic rates of return.
They are biased upward, more for some industries than for others, because of the conservative approach of accountants who do

[18]"The Great Alaskan Oil Freeze," *Business Week,* February 26, 1979, p. 74.

[19]Stigler, *Capital and Rates of Return in Manufacturing* (Princeton: Princeton
University Press, 1963), pp. 3–6.

[20]This is the only alleged evidence offered by the Neal Commission for its conten-
tion that high concentration is an index to oligopoly. "... studies have found a
close association between high levels of concentration and persistently high rates
of return on capital..." "Task Force Report on Antitrust Policy," *Trade Regulation Reports,* p. II–8.

[21]Stigler, *Capital and Rates of Return,* p. 5.

[22]For some exceptions, see William Jordan, "Producer Protection, Prior Market
Structure, and the Effects of Government Regulation," *Journal of Law & Economics* 15 (April 1972): 151–76.

not capitalize several types of investment (spending on research, advertising, development of dealer networks, training of the work force, breaking-in plant), do not revalue assets after the occurrence of inflation, and write off investment in the projects that fail.[23] Accounting rates of return are biased downward in rapidly growing industries, in which a large proportion of assets are new, relative to rates of return in slowly growing or declining industries, in which a large proportion of assets are more fully depreciated.[24]

Professor Fritz Machlup warns us as follows:

> Although many monopolistic firms may make profits, there are several fundamental pitfalls in the idea that the accounting rate of profit can show the degree to which monopoly power is exercised.
>
> That the accounting rates of profit, the only ones that may be available to the statistician, are such unreliable indices of economic excess profits and monopoly situations is unfortunate, since the relationship between supernormal profits and monopolistic barriers against potential entrants into the industry is highly significant. Firms sheltered against newcomers' competition are likely to earn higher returns on their investments than firms in industries wide open to anybody willing to start a new business.
>
> Before results of investigations of "adjusted profit rates" become available we cannot say whether and how it will be possible to separate monopoly elements. But we know for certain that such a separation is not possible on the basis of the unadjusted accounting rates of profit and that these rates cannot be accepted as a measurement of the degree of monopoly.[25]

For what the data may be worth, let us examine trends in the accounting returns on net worth in leading manufacturing corporations grouped by industry. If returns remain high in high-return industries and low in low-return industries without being demonstrably the result of arbitrary accounting conventions, then we can at least say that we have failed to show that manufacturing is not monopolized. The implication would follow that Galbraith *may* be correct in saying that each of the 500 biggest industrial companies controls its market and that U.S. markets are monopolized, at least in the case of manufactured products. If, however, high rates of return erode and low returns improve, with returns

[23]Stigler, "A Note on Profitability, Competition, and Concentration," in *The Organization of Industry* (Homewood, Ill.: Richard D. Irwin, 1968), p. 142.

[24]Y. Brozen, "The Significance of Profit Data for Antitrust Policy," *Antitrust Bulletin* (Spring 1969): 119–39.

[25]F. Machlup, *The Political Economy of Monopoly* (Baltimore: Johns Hopkins University Press, 1952), p. 493.

converging on the average rate, then we may be entitled to suspect that the market is competitive. We may assert that the market does manage to force a reallocation of resources to the goods most preferred by consumers and away from the production of less preferable goods, and the assertion will rest on better evidence than simple absolute or relative size of firms.

What the Data Show

Let us examine the top earning industries of 1948, a cycle peak year, using the data for leading corporations grouped by industry. Then let us look at their ranks eight years later, the next year in which a cyclical peak occurred without the distortions introduced by price controls. Doing this, we find that the top 20 out of 40 industries ranked by earnings in 1948 fell in average rank in the next eight years. They ended in 1956 with a random distribution among the 40 ranks, ranging from fourth to bottom rank instead of top to middle rank (see table 1). The average earnings rank among the 1948 top 20 dropped to very near the average for all 40 industries (from an average rank of 10.5 to 19.6). Similarly, the average industry in the bottom half did not remain in the middle of the bottom half. Its rate of return rank rose from the average for the bottom half to very near the average for all the industries ranked (from 30.5 to 21.4). This is exactly what is supposed not to occur in monopolized markets. What happened is what we would expect in a group of competitive industries.

TABLE 1

RETURN ON NET WORTH IN LEADING MANUFACTURING
CORPORATIONS AND RANK BY INDUSTRY GROUP,
1948 AND 1956

Industry (and no. of firms)			Return on Book Net Worth		Rank by Book Return	
	1948	1956	1948	1956	1948	1956
Lumber	29	26	29.3%	12.6%	1	20
Appliances	45	36	26.6	12.1	2	25
Textiles	126	80	26.2	6.6	3	39.5
Auto and trucks	28	14	26.0	14.6	4	12.5
Distilling	12	12	24.8	6.8	5	38

(Cont.)

TABLE 1 *(Cont.)*

Industry (and no. of firms)			Return on Book Net Worth		Rank by Book Return	
	1948	1956	1948	1956	1948	1956
Office equipment	27	27	24.3%	17.5%	6	7.5
Auto parts	68	57	23.5	13.3	7	19
Brewing	31	24	22.8	8.1	8	35
Petroleum products	44	116	22.1	14.6	9	12.5
Baking	24	18	21.4	12.2	10	22.5
Drugs, soap, cosmetics	32	46	21.3	19.9	11	4
Building & plumbing equipment	77	81	21.0	11.2	12	30
Soft drinks	17	15	20.4	13.9	13.5	14.5
Pulp and paper	85	73	20.4	13.8	13.5	16.5
Electrical equipment, radio, TV	80	97	20.3	11.8	15	27.5
Machinery	166	168	18.6	14.9	16	11
Furniture	18	19	18.3	11.8	17	27.5
Other stone, clay	45	55	18.2	15.8	18	9
Total Mfg.			18.2	13.9		
Chemicals	65	69	17.7	15.5	19.5	10
Other metal products	94	112	17.7	12.1	19.5	25
Cement	31	30	17.0	20.6	21	2
Other food	82	88	16.9	11.7	22	29
Hardware & tools	47	51	16.3	12.2	23	22.5
Glass	13	18	15.5	17.7	24	6
Nonferrous metals	34	46	14.9	17.8	25	5
Shoes	25	25	14.7	10.3	26	32
Printing & publishing	34	42	14.3	13.8	27.5	16.5
Tobacco products	23	20	14.3	12.1	27.5	25
Tires, rubber products	25	29	14.0	13.6	29	18
Iron and steel	54	56	13.9	13.9	30	14.5
Apparel	33	49	13.8	7.8	31	36
Agricultural implements	12	10	13.6	8.3	32.5	34
Leather	9		13.6	10.8	32.5	31
Paint	19	22	13.1	17.5	34	7.5
Dairy products	18	12	13.0	12.4	35	21
Sugar	23	23	12.2	6.6	36	39.5
Shipbuilding	6	8	11.7	20.0	37	3
Railway equipment	27	21	9.2	9.9	38	33
Meat packing	21	15	7.2	7.7	39	37
Aircraft	27	41	2.9	21.4	40	1

NOTE: The average rank of the industries may be summarized as follows:

	Average Rank	
	1948	1956
Industries 1–20 (1948)	10.5	19.6
Industries 21–40 (1948)	30.5	21.4
All Industries	20.5	20.5

SOURCE: First National City Bank Monthly Economic Letter, April 1949 and 1950, and April 1957 and 1958

That this result is not peculiar to the period is demonstrated by examining the behavior of the ranks of 40 industries from 1966 to 1978. The average industry in the 1966 top 20 dropped from a 10.5 rank in 1966 to 18.1 in 1978. The average industry in the 1966 bottom 20 rose from a 30.5 rank in 1966 to 22.9 in 1978 (table 2).

TABLE 2

RETURN ON NET WORTH IN LEADING MANUFACTURING
CORPORATIONS AND RANK BY INDUSTRY GROUP,
1966 AND 1978
(return measured on beginning of year net worth)

Industry (and no. of firms)			Return on Book Net Worth		Rank by Book Return	
	1966	1978	1966	1978	1966	1978
Soft drinks	17	14	22.0%	22.8%	1	1
Instrum. & photo goods	114	98	21.2	19.1	2	11
Drugs & medicines	39	28	21.0	21.5	3	4
Hardware & tools	44	22	19.2	18.4	4	12.5
Office equipment, computers	51	58	18.1	22.5	5.5	2
Printing & publishing	89	55	18.1	18.4	5.5	12.5
Soaps, cosmetics	34	30	17.9	20.8	7	5
Autos & trucks	15	7	17.8	17.2	8	18
Electrical equipment, radio, TV	339	159	16.7	18.0	9	15
Machinery	210	113	16.0	17.0	10	19
Clothing & apparel	85	57	15.9	14.7	11	27
Aircraft & space	55	28	15.7	19.7	12.5	9
Nonferrous metals	66	27	15.7	10.2	12.5	36
Chemical	79	51	15.1	15.0	14	26
Appliances	21	13	15.0	15.7	15	24
Agricultural implements, construction equipment	44	39	14.7	18.3	16	14
Auto parts	41	29	14.5	17.8	17	16
Furniture	37	29	14.2	9.6	18	38
Other metal products	63	75	14.0	13.6	19	31.5
Paint & varnish	22	10	13.9	8.1	20.5	40
Total Mfg.			14.2	15.9		
Baking	15	10	13.9	20.1	20.5	6
Tobacco products	12	9	13.8	19.8	22	7
Other food	84	34	13.3	16.5	23	20
Shoes, leather	25	16	13.1	16.3	24	22
Tires, rubber products	58	32	13.0	16.2	25	23
Brewing	17	8	12.8	11.4	26	34
Glass	15	14	12.7	13.6	27	31.5
Petroleum products, refineries	106	94	12.6	14.3	28	28

(Cont.)

TABLE 2 *(Cont.)*

Industry (and no. of firms)			Return on Book Net Worth		Rank by Book Return	
	1966	1978	1966	1978	1966	1978
Dairy products	13	7	12.4%	15.6%	29	25
Miscellaneous manufacturing	99	37	12.1	16.4	30	21
Textile products	70	42	11.9	9.6	31.5	38
Building & plumbing equipment	60	13	11.9	21.8	31.5	3
Paper	75	47	11.8	14.0	33	30
Lumber & wood products	27	34	11.0	19.7	34	9
Distilling	13	6	10.6	14.2	35	29
Iron & steel	82	55	9.3	9.6	36	38
Other stone, clay	44	28	9.2	17.5	37	17
Sugar	15	14	9.1	12.0	38	33
Cement	17	10	7.0	19.7	39	9
Meat packing	27	20	5.5	10.5	40	35

	Average Rank	
	1966	1978
Industries 1–20 (1966)	10.5	18.1
Industries 21–40 (1966)	30.5	22.9
All Industries	20.5	20.5

Inasmuch as 1948, 1956, 1966, and 1978 were all years in which the business cycle peaked, it is surprising to find such marked convergence of industry profitability ranks. Cyclically sensitive industries, such as autos and machinery, tend to have high returns in prosperous years (and low returns in depressed years). They would be top-ranked industries in these peak years. As a result, we would not expect the average ranks of the top and bottom groups of industries to converge as completely as they did from one prosperous year to another. That they did so despite the use of only prosperous years (and accounting rates of return) for the comparison is strong evidence of an absence of pervasive monopoly. As the White House Antitrust Task Force pointed out, "the persistence of high profits over extended time periods and over whole industries... suggest artificial restraints on output and the absence of fully effective competition."[26] But persistence of high profits did *not* occur.

---

[26] "Task Force Report on Antitrust Policy."

While the pattern of shifting rate-of-return-ranks among manufacturing industries provides evidence that production ebbs and flows are dictated by competitive markets, the question might still be raised whether the pattern differs between concentrated and diffused industries. Stigler hypothesizes as follows:

> Competitive industries will have a volatile pattern of rates of return, for the movements into high-profit industries and out of low-profit industries will—together with the flow of new disturbances of equilibrium—lead to a constantly changing hierarchy of rates of return. In the monopolistic industries, on the other hand, the usually profitable industries will be able to preserve their preferential position for considerable periods of time.[27]

If concentrated industries are difficult to enter and firms in concentrated industries restrain output to maintain profitability—that is, if monopoly and concentration are correlated—we can expect less scrambling of profit ranks among concentrated industries in successive years than in diffused industries. In the latter—if atomism and competition are correlated—attractive profits induce entry and expansion by resident firms. This process erodes high profits and drops the rank of the relatively higher profit industries, thus causing an increasing scrambling of industry profitablity ranks as time is allowed for the reallocation of resources in response to the attraction of profits and random disturbances of equilibrium.

For the 1919–1928 period, the correlation of profit ranks for successive years in concentrated industries (four-firm concentration ratio 60 percent or greater) is significantly *poorer* than in the unconcentrated (less than 50 percent concentrated) or ambiguous (50 to 60 percent concentrated) sets of industries (table 4). Monopoly was not a correlate of concentration in that period. In the 1947–1957 period, the correlations in the concentrated and unconcentrated sets are not significantly different until we reach those between rates of return separated by seven years. Then they become significantly poorer in the concentrated industries (table 3). In the 1958–1968 period, the correlations are significantly better in the concentrated than the unconcentrated until eight years after any given year.

---

[27]Stigler, *Capital and Rates of Return,* p. 70.

TABLE 3

INTERTEMPORAL CORRELATION OF RATES OF RETURN
FOR CONCENTRATED, UNCONCENTRATED AND AMBIGUOUS INDUSTRIES,
1919–28, 1947–57, AND 1958–68

	Average Correlations		
Industry Structure	1919–28[a]	1947–57[b]	1958–68[b]
	Rates of Return in Year T and (T+1)		
Concentrated	0.51	0.74	0.88
Unconcentrated	.64	.63	.83
Ambiguous	.85	.82	.86
	Rates of Return in Year T and (T+2)		
Concentrated	.42	.59	.80
Unconcentrated	.57	.49	.66
Ambiguous	.77	.70	.71
	Rates of Return in Year T and (T+3)		
Concentrated	.29	.54	.74
Unconcentrated	.54	.49	.41
Ambiguous	.63	.67	.69
	Rates of Return in Year T and (T+4)		
Concentrated	.17	.50	.70
Unconcentrated	.45	.50	.49
Ambiguous	.50	.68	.66
	Rates of Return in Year T and (T+5)		
Concentrated	.15	.47	.65
Unconcentrated	.31	.39	.34
Ambiguous	.46	.60	.54
	Rates of Return in Year T and (T+6)		
Concentrated	.13	.29	.55
Unconcentrated	.26	.27	.22
Ambiguous	.41	.52	.61
	Rates of Return in Year T and (T+7)		
Concentrated	− .02	.16	.46
Unconcentrated	.13	.47	.13
Ambiguous	.47	.43	.54
	Rates of Return in Year T and (T+8)		
Concentrated	− .02	.18	.39
Unconcentrated	.29	.38	.33
Ambiguous	.50	.42	.50
	Rates of Return in Year T and (T+9)		
Concentrated	− .25	.17	.46
Unconcentrated	.08	.22	.34
Ambiguous	.31	.34	.52

(Cont.)

TABLE 3 *(Cont.)*

[a] Calculated by Aldy Keene from data on earnings on equity for 2,046 identical leading corporations classified in 72 industries reported in Ralph C. Epstein, *Industrial Profits in the United States* (1934). Concentration classification according to data in National Resources Committee, *The Structure of the American Economy* (June 1939). Classification scheme that used by G. J. Stigler, *Capital and Rates of Return in Manufacturing Industries* (1963).

[b] James C. Ellert, *Concentration, Disequilibria, and the Convergence Pattern in Industry Rates of Return* (multilith, 1971). Compustat data for 565 corporations classified in 141 industries used.

Can we take this to mean that concentrated industries were more competitive than the diffused industries until 1958 and then became less competitive? There is no direct evidence suggesting greater (or less) competitiveness in concentrated industries in the two earlier periods. There was greater cyclical instability in the two earlier periods and Qualls found greater cyclical instability of price-cost margins in concentrated than in diffused industries.[28] This is, perhaps, the explanation for the difference in the latter period from the two earlier.

Another explanation can be offered with some slight supporting evidence. Unrecorded intangible capital is, on average, relatively greater in recent times in concentrated than in unconcentrated industries. Telser found that concentrated industries invest more in human capital than the unconcentrated.[29] Since training programs within industry have been growing relative to other magnitudes in the economy in the postwar period, it would appear that this unrecorded asset may more and more be biasing accounting rates of return upward in some concentrated industries by varying amounts, thus causing a spurious recent stability in the pattern of relative profitability in concentrated industries. In other words, some industry rates of return are pushed upward more than others by the accounting bias. Hence, the range in which an industry profit rate moves is separated from the range of

[28] P. D. Qualls, *Market Structure and Price—Cost Margin Flexibility in American Manufacturing, 1958–70,* FTC Special Paper (March 1977).

[29] L. Telser, "Some Determinants of Returns to Manufacturing Industries," in *Competition, Collusion, and Game Theory* (Chicago: Aldine Atherton, 1972), p. 312.

movement in other industries. A spurious stability in the relative rank of the industry's return results.

A hypothetical example may help clarify the issue. Suppose an industry, half of whose assets consists of unrecorded intangibles, reports a 20 percent return while another with no intangibles reports an 8 percent return. If current outlays on intangible investments (which are expensed) equal depreciation of unrecorded intangibles, then the true return in the first industry is 10 percent (assuming no other accounting biases). Now suppose that events occur which reduce returns in the high accounting return industry by half and in the low return industry by one-quarter. The reported returns will show the first industry earning 10 percent and the second 6. The first industry will continue in its number one rank and the second in number two, and the correlation of ranks will be persistent. If rates of return were not differentially biased by the accounting treatment of intangible outlays, however, the first industry would sink from a 10 to 5 percent rate of return while the second sinks from 8 to 6 percent. The ranks of the two would reverse and the pattern of relative profitability would not show the spurious stability that is caused by differential accounting biases.

The pharmaceutical industry provides an example of the spurious stability in rank and persistence of a high accounting rate of return caused by the omission of a major portion of an industry's capital from its accounting statements. It is the most research-intensive industry in the American economy and one of the most promotion-intensive. Since research and information providing activities are expensed as incurred, despite the returns appearing in later accounting periods, its book capital understates its actual capital by a larger proportion than in any other industry. As a result, its accounting rate of return is high and the industry ranks among the top three most of the time in the forty-industry list used in table 2. In the last three decades (1950–1978), it was number one on the list 6 times, number two 9 times, and number three 6 times. It did not drop below number ten at any time.

A recomputation of the drug industry rate of return by Professor Kenneth Clarkson, capitalizing research and the advertising portion of promotion expenditures, dropped the industry's average return for 1959–1973 from 18.3 to 12.9 percent, the largest drop among the eleven industries for which Clarkson recomputed rates of return. The average decline in the other industries was 1.2 percentage points as compared to the 5.4 point drop in pharmaceuticals.[30] The industry consistently ranks high, then, simply because accounting conventions cause a much larger departure of the accounting from the economic rate of return than in any other industry.

Other evidence also points to the fact that the high rank of the drug industry and its persistence was spurious. The number of pharmaceutical firms dropped from 1,123 in 1947 to 680 in 1972. This occurred despite a very rapid growth in sales from $0.9 billion in 1947 to $7.1 billion in 1972. If the industry were truly as profitable as indicated by the accounting rate of return, firms would not have been departing as rapidly as they did unless the dispersion in rates of return among firms was unusually large, indicating an unusually risky industry with many firms failing while others did unusually well. If the latter were the situation, then the high returns could encompass a risk premium with the risk-adjusted rate of return being below average.[31]

Has American Manufacturing Grown Less Competitive?

The great merger wave at the end of the nineteenth century involved a proportion of manufacturing assets which has never been remotely approached in all mergers combined in the several decades since. According to some authors, the consolidations of that time and of the twenties set an oligopolistic stamp on American manufacturing which makes it noncompetitive by comparison with the atomistic structure of the pre-1890 era.[32]

In contrast to this view, Professor Ambrose Winston observed that

> ... competition has in our day become intense and swift and sure beyond all previous human experience.
> What do we mean by competition? We ought to mean the ready movement of the factors of production—labor or productive instruments—toward those employments in which prices are exceptionally high and profits large. That is, competition is substantially "mobility." ...

[30]K. Clarkson, *Intangible Capital and Rates of Return* (Washington, D.C.: American Enterprise Institute for Public Policy Research, 1977), p. 64, table 16.
[31]Brozen, "Foreword," in Clarkson, *Intangible Capital,* pp. 11-16.
[32]Shepherd, *Economics of Industrial Organization,* p. 207.

> New capital—the current accumulation of surplus income—is unspecialized industrial protoplasm quickly turning in any direction, attracted by the hope of profit, creating new competing products with a promptness and certainty unknown in the age of handicraft.
>
> The owners of investment capital and their advisers are looking incessantly for the most profitable opportunities for its employment. The earnings from oil, from steel, from the packing industry, from automobiles, from sugar, from commerce and shipping, flow into steel or automobiles or oil, or whatever gives greatest promise of high earnings.[33]

We used the test of competition proposed by Professor Winston in examining the rate at which industries ranked high or low by profitability converged on the middle rank. We saw the average rank of the top-ranked industries of 1948 move 91 percent of the distance toward the average rank by 1956 (table 1). The top-ranked industries of 1966 moved 76 percent of the distance toward an average rank by 1978 (table 2) despite the tendency of cyclical industries to be in a top rank in all such years as 1948, 1956, 1966, and 1978. By performing a similar test on pre-1890 manufacturing industries, perhaps we can judge whether the alleged oligopolization of manufacturing has occurred, ending an idyllic, competitive era.

Professors Atack, Bateman, and Weiss have extracted profitability data from the 1850, 1860, and 1870 Manuscript Censuses. Using the twenty-one industries for which they computed returns, we find that the top-ranked industries of 1850 moved only 36 percent of the distance toward an average rank by 1860 (table 4), half the rate of movement that occurred in recent years. And this was no outlier of monopolistic rigidity. The movement of the top-ranked group of 1860 toward an average rank went only 52 percent of the distance between 1860 and 1870 (table 5) despite enormous economic shocks and random disturbances of equilibrium positions in the Civil War and Reconstruction era.

It seems that there was less fluidity in "industrial protoplasm" in the days before the rise of large corporations and "dominant" firms than there has been since. If anything, the American manufacturing economy is more competitive today than ever before, if we can judge by these data.

---

[33]A. P. Winston, "The Chimera of Monopoly," *The Atlantic Monthly,* November 1924; reprinted in *The Freeman,* September 1960.

TABLE 4

PROFIT RATE IN UNITED STATES MANUFACTURING
BY MAJOR INDUSTRIES, 1850–1860

Industry	Profit Rate		Profit Rank	
	1850	1860	1850	1860
Blacksmithing	39.5%	30.2%	1	6
Tin, copper, & sheet iron	35.4	22.8	2	12
Saddlery	33.5	39.7	3	2
Printing	33.1	31.3	4	4
Books and shoes	31.8	34.1	5	3
Meat packing	29.0	42.7	6	1
All Industries	26.1	25.9		
Furniture	25.1	21.1	7	14.5
Agricultural implements	23.0	21.3	8	13
Leather	22.7	23.4	9	9
Lumber milling	22.4	23.3	10	10.5
Floor milling	22.1	23.3	11	10.5
Pig Iron	22.0	9.2	12	21
Cast iron	21.8	24.2	13	7
Wagons & carriages	21.6	23.8	14	8
Machinery	16.8	31.0	15	5
Cooperage	14.2	19.1	16	18
Clothing	12.9	21.1	17	14.5
Woolen textiles	10.0	20.6	18	17
Brick making	0.8	13.5	19.5	20
Bar iron	0.8	21.0	19.5	16
Cotton textiles	0.2	13.6	21	19

SOURCE: Jeremy Atack, Fred Bateman, and Thomas Weiss, *Risk, the Rate of Return and the Pattern of Investment in Nineteenth Century American Industrialization* (May 25, 1979).

	1850	1860	1870
Industries 1–11 (1850)	6.0	7.8	8.0
Industries 11–21 (1850)	16.0	14.2	14.0
All industries	11.0	11.0	11.0

TABLE 5

PROFIT RATE IN UNITED STATES MANUFACTURING
BY MAJOR INDUSTRIES, 1860–1870

Industry	Profit Rate		Profit Rank	
	1860	1870	1860	1870
Meat packing	42.7%	63.1%	1	1
Saddlery	39.7	38.5	2	4
Books and shoes	34.1	62.0	3	2
Printing	31.3	32.2	4	5
Machinery	31.0	18.5	5	14.5
Blacksmithing	30.2	55.2	6	3
All Industries	25.9	29.3		
Cast iron	24.2	18.0	7	16
Wagons & carriages	23.8	25.7	8	9
Leather	23.4	21.3	9	11
Lumber milling	23.3	17.3	10.5	17
Flour milling	23.3	19.3	10.5	13
Tin, copper, & sheet iron	22.8	28.4	12	7
Agricultural implements	21.3	12.4	13	19
Furniture	21.1	31.0	14.5	6
Clothing	21.1	27.0	14.5	8
Bar iron	21.0	5.1	16	20
Woolen textiles	20.6	14.0	17	18
Cooperage	19.1	21.8	18	10
Cotton textiles	13.6	18.5	19	14.5
Brick making	13.5	20.6	20	12
Pig iron	9.2	-1.6	21	21

NOTE: The average rank of the industries may be summarized as follows:

	Average Rank	
	1860	1870
Industries 1–11 (1860)	6.0	8.6
Industries 11–21 (1860)	16.0	13.7
All industries	11.0	11.0

Conclusion

The effort devoted to monopoly in manufacturing appears to be in inverse proportion to the triviality of the problem. Monopoly in manufacturing has received inordinate attention largely because of a misplaced faith in concentration ratios as an index of monopoly and because big companies, which are always suspect, abound in this sector. Every attempt to measure monopoly misallocation in manufacturing has indicated that the degree is slight even when using the most unfavorable assumptions as to the meaning of the data employed.[34]

Those concerned with the monopoly problem in the United States tend to neglect the important monopolies which cause a more than trivial misallocation of resources. The Airline Pilot's Association, which by creating a monopoly of pilots supplied to scheduled airlines has won returns on private investment in pilot training far exceeding those earned by any group of corporations in any of the SIC industries, is seldom studied.[35] The legislative and regulatory support given to cartels in agriculture, transportation, and trades such as barbering and drug retailing receives little or no attention in the collections of readings on the monopoly problem. The monopoly problem is far from trivial in the non-manufacturing areas of the economy and in the small firm industries such as taxi operation,[36] yet it receives little attention in comparison to the effort devoted to manufacturing.

[34]A. Harberger, "Monopoly and Resource Allocation," *American Economic Review* 44 (May 1954): 77–87; D. Schwartzman, "The Effect of Monopoly on Price," *Journal of Political Economy* 67 (August 1959): 361.

[35]The only study of the Air Line Pilots' Association monopoly return is that by S. Sobotka, *Economic Implications of Jet Operations* (Evanston, Ill.: Transportation Center, 1958). He found that the monopolized sector of airline piloting provided a lifetime income whose present value, at that time, exceeded the present value of pilots' lifetime earnings in less monopolized sectors by 32% with duty hours required in the monopolized sector amounting to only 50% of the duty hours required in the less monopolized sector.

[36]The capitalized value of the monopoly return in the New York City taxicab industry alone exceeds $600 million.

The Attack on Concentration

The task of antitrust is to identify and prohibit those forms of behavior whose net effect is output-restricting and hence detrimental.
—Robert Bork, *The Antitrust Paradox*
(1978), p.122.

No field in the industrial organization literature has been as well
plowed as the relationship between concentration and profitability.... (D)espite its bulk, the literature fails to inform us how to
interpret its main findings.... (I)f concentration and profitability
are indeed related, what market process produces the relationship?
The traditional answer has been that high concentration facilitates
collusion.... Unfortunately, this answer does not logically follow
from the usual evidence, so its acceptance by economists and practitioners of antitrust policy is little more than an act of faith.
—Sam Peltzman, "The Gains and Losses
from Industrial Concentration,"
Journal of Law and Economics
(1977), p. 229.

There is a strange notion brewing in the Antitrust Division and the
Federal Trade Commission—a notion that will be suicidal for the
country if we adopt it.* It is the notion that we must penalize any
firm (or small group of firms) that, by operating efficiently and
producing greater values for consumers, wins a large share of the
market. Perhaps that notion emerges from the passion for equali-
ty of results that has come to pervade public policy; perhaps it is
simply envy; or perhaps it is the final erosion, perversion, or
transmutation of democracy from individual sovereignty into
mobocracy—tyranny by majority.

Whatever the roots of the strange flowers now blooming in the
fields of antitrust, the fact is that the antitrust agencies are attempting to remake antitrust law to penalize success in serving

*This paper was presented before the Ashland, Kentucky, Economic Club, Sep-
tember 15, 1978.

consumers. Next to the Occupational Safety and Health Administration, the old Interstate Commerce Commission, and the Civil Aeronautics Board, the most anticonsumer agency in Washington[1] is the FTC.[2]

Once we gave high regard to those who created great enterprises by designing desirable products, producing them at low cost, and offering them at such attractive prices that they won a large body of customers. Henry Ford in his day was looked upon as an industrial hero. Today, he would be regarded as a monopolizing fiend upon whom the antitrust prosecutors should be unleashed. The 1921 Ford Company, with its more than 60 percent share of the market, would today be called a dominant firm and charged with violating the antitrust laws.

Just a few months ago, an antitrust complaint was served upon Du Pont because it developed a low-cost method for producing titanium dioxide pigments. There was no objection to the development of a lower-cost method of production, but Du Pont made the fatal error of passing enough of the cost saving on to buyers to win 40 percent of the market served by domestic producers. Not only did it do that but it is going to enlarge its capacity, building a new plant at De Lisle, Mississippi, in order to serve even more customers (who also would like to obtain domestic titanium dioxide at low cost). Can you imagine that any enterprise would engage in such a nefarious activity? It should, according to the FTC, behave like a monopolist. It should restrict its output, instead of expanding, and charge higher prices (and let the business go to foreign firms).

Antitrust Upside Down

That is a total perversion of the intent of our antitrust law. If the FTC is not standing antitrust law on its head, then I simply do not understand what our antitrust law says. The words "every con-

[1]Robert S. Smith, *The Occupational Safety and Health Act: Its Goals and Its Achievements* (Washington, D.C.: American Enterprise Institute, 1976); Thomas Moore, *Freight Transportation Regulation: Surface Freight and the ICC* (Washington, D.C.: American Enterprise Institute, 1975). See also the evaluations by the U.S. Council on Wage and Price Stability of various OSHA standards.

[2]For an example of the FTC's anticonsumer actions, see W. Liebeler, "Toward a Consumer's Antitrust Law: The Federal Trade Commission and Vertical Mergers

tract, combination, or conspiracy, in restraint of trade is hereby declared to be illegal'' say that it is *restraint of output* that is in violation of the law. But the FTC contends that Du Pont is violating the law because it has "adopted and implemented a plan to *expand* its domestic production capacity."[3] That quite plainly says that the FTC regards Du Pont as breaking the law by *expanding* trade. Is that what the law says is illegal?

In whatever way I torture the phrases in the antitrust law, I simply cannot get it to say that expanding trade is illegal despite the thunder in the FTC complaint. Whenever anyone builds more capacity and uses it to produce more product, more trade must result. I can't believe that Du Pont is building a new titanium dioxide plant just because it wants a handsome monument at which to gaze—and neither does the FTC. What the FTC is complaining about is that Du Pont intends to produce TiO_2 in its new plant and increase its sales—and it is nasty of Du Pont to have already built enough plants to take care of 40 percent of the needs of customers for a domestic product. That makes Du Pont "the nation's dominant producer."[4] There can hardly be anything more venal than a "dominant producer," unless it is a "shared monopoly."

"Shared monopoly" sounds like a label for a conspiracy among several firms to monopolize a market and share the fruits of that monopoly. But that is not what the FTC means by the label. The phrase is FTC code for a few firms winning and holding a large share of the business in some product line. The FTC staff is currently prosecuting Kellogg, General Foods, and General Mills for "sharing a monopoly" of ready-to-eat (RTE) cereals. These three firms have managed to produce and distribute cereals that taste good enough and cost consumers little enough to win more than three-quarters of the RTE business. That is their crime.

Did these three firms conspire with each other to somehow force other firms out of the industry and then conspire to reduce supplies and raise prices? The FTC disavows any accusation of any such conspiracy. It says that the crime of which these firms

---

in the Cement Industry," *UCLA Law Review* 15 (June 1968): 1153–1202. See also Robert Bork, "The Supreme Court vs. Corporate Efficiency," *Fortune,* August 1967, pp. 92–93.

[3]*FTC News Summary,* April 14, 1978, p. 1. Emphasis added.

[4]Ibid.

are guilty is "brand proliferation." The heinous conduct of which it accuses these firms is that of trying to give consumers what they want. It is now a crime, that is, the FTC is trying to make it a crime, to follow that old merchandising maxim for success, "Give the lady what she wants."

The cereal companies should have stuck to producing corn flakes. Never mind the demand for a bran cereal, or a high protein cereal, or a vitamin-enriched cereal, or a presweetened cereal. Anyway, says the FTC in its complaint, there are no differences between cereals—except those artificially created in the minds of consumers by hypnotizing them with advertising.[5] Of course, if the new brands offered by the three firms in the 1950s and 1960s had not won a large share of the market, nothing would have been wrong with "brand proliferation." But the new brands pleased consumers. They won for the three firms a large share of the market. That, at bottom, is the crime these firms committed. The RTE cereal industry has become "concentrated," that is, most of the sales in the industry are made by a few firms. That is a condition which neither the FTC nor the Antitrust Division intends to tolerate.

The FTC staff has also accused the eight major petroleum refiners of engaging in a "shared monopoly" in the petroleum refining industry. It is asking that these corporations be broken into smaller companies. The major crime of which the Big Eight stand accused is that of maintaining a "noncompetitive market structure." This phrase is never cogently defined by the FTC staff, but "concentration" seems to be the nub of it. Complaint counsel says the eight companies "are all vertically integrated firms with *substantial horizontal concentration* at every level of the industry" (emphasis added).[6] Counsel also says the eight "own and operate refineries accounting for approximately 65 percent of rated crude oil refining capacity in the relevant market." Even more damning:

> This figure...understates concentration...because [the eight firms]...utilize more of their refining capacity than other refiners. Hence [their] share of *production* of refined petroleum products...is higher than their share of rated refinery capacity....[7]

[5]FTC Docket No. 8883, April 26, 1972.

[6]Complaint Counsel's Prediscovery Statement, In the Matter of Exxon Corporation, et al., Docket No. 8934, p. 7.

[7]Ibid., pp. 9–10.

Again, here is the accusation that these alleged monopolists are not behaving like monopolists. Instead of restricting output and restraining trade, they push their capacity harder than do their competitors and expand output and trade. Apparently they are unaware of the fact that they are monopolists who can get higher prices by restricting output. Again, the FTC is displeased by efforts to expand trade and is standing antitrust law on its head by saying that the *failure to restrict trade* is a violation of the law. The FTC even accuses the companies of building pipelines to provide themselves with "cheap transportation."[8] Again, as in titanium dioxide, it is apparently illegal to reduce costs and pass enough of these cost savings on to customers to win an appreciable share of the market. (In the petroleum case, we cannot say a "large" share of the market has been won since no petroleum refining firm sells as much as 10 percent of the petroleum products sold in the United States.)

These three cases are cited to show the current state of antitrust doctrine at the antitrust agencies. The question remains of whether the courts will buy this upside-down view of antitrust law in view of its legislative history.[9]

Antitrust Not Intended to Fragment Industry

When federal antitrust policy began, with the signing of the Sherman Act in 1890, it was aimed at benefiting consumers. In the words of Senator Sherman, the act was to outlaw arrangements "designed, or which tend, to advance the cost to the customer." It was intended neither to fragment industry nor to prevent occupancy of a major share of a market by one or a few firms.[10] When

---

[8] Ibid., p. 8. In the Alice-in-Wonderland economics of the Antitrust Division, a new doctrine is currently being propounded. The companies building the pipelines, says the Antitrust Division, "undersized" them to prevent cheap transportation from being available to competitors. These companies should have built bigger pipelines to provide cheap transportation for yet undiscovered crude to not-yet-planned refineries without any guarantees or firm prospects that the extra capacity would be utilized.

[9] The Court did accept this upside-down view in reversing the lower court in the Alcoa case. See Y. Brozen, "Antitrust out of Hand," *The Conference Board Record* 11 (March 1974): 14–18.

[10] Neither was the Federal Trade Commission Act intended for this purpose. See Layne E. Kruse, "Deconcentration and Section 5 of the Federal Trade Commission Act," *George Washington Law Review* 46 (January 1978): 200–32.

Senator George Hoar explained to the Senate the Judiciary Committee's final draft of the bill, he declared that *a man who "got the whole business because nobody could do it as well as he could" would not be in violation of the Sherman Act.* As Professor Bork has pointed out in his examination of Sherman Act legislative history, "The statute was intended to strike at cartels, horizontal mergers of monopolistic proportions, and predatory business tactics."[11] As the act itself says, "Every conspiracy in *restraint* of trade...is hereby declared illegal" (emphasis added).

Cost and price reductions and product improvements by a firm expand the trade of a whole industry. Since firms doing this frequently win a large share of the markets in which they operate, judges in the early days of antitrust litigation did not hold "concentration" of sales in the hands of a few firms or "dominance" by a single firm to be illegal in and of itself. Standard Oil and American Tobacco were broken up in 1911 because they had been built by a very large number of mergers of monopolistic proportions with wrongful intent and had then engaged in "acts and dealings wholly inconsistent with the theory that they were made with the single conception of advancing the development of business...by usual methods...." The defendants failed to show that the intent underlying their mergers and their acts was the normal one of efficiency and expansion of trade—they failed to show "countervailing circumstances" in Judge White's phrase. They were, therefore, subjected to antitrust remedies. The remedies were not applied because of their dominance but because they were formed and maintained by *monopolizing* acts and intent—that is, by a desire to gain *control* of the supply of a product and to use that control to charge a monopoly price and thereby restrain trade.

Dominant Firms Do Not Control Supply and Price

There is a distinction between *controlling* the supply of a product and *producing* or selling most of the supply of a product. "Dominant" producers who *sell* a major portion of a product's supply

---

[11]Robert Bork, *The Antitrust Paradox: A Policy at War with Itself* (New York: Basic Books, Inc, 1978), p. 20.

usually have no control over the supply. They have no power to set any lower level of industry output and a higher price than that which would prevail in a market with many suppliers and no dominant firm. Usually, a dominant producer is the most efficient firm in the industry.[12] Its large output is the result of its efficiency in supplying the market. The market price is as low as it would be with many producers—frequently lower.[13] Any attempt by a dominant firm to restrict its own supply and increase price after reaching a "dominant" position simply results in the expansion of output by other firms, the entry of additional firms, and loss of its dominance. A dominant firm can keep its dominance only by behaving competitively. *The fact that there is a dominant firm (or small group of firms) in an industry is evidence of competitive behavior—not of monopolization.*[14]

The lack of ability of a dominant firm (or group of firms) to control supply and price simply because it produces a major part of the supply of a product is illustrated by the experience of the automobile industry in 1927. From 1921 to 1925 the Ford Motor Company supplied more automobiles than all other firms combined. The Ford Company was a dominant firm. It completely shut off its supply to the market for nearly the entire year in 1927 when it closed to retool for the change from the Model T to the Model A. If the fact that a firm supplies the majority of a market gives it any power to control supply and price, then the complete withdrawal of that firm's supply should certainly cause a rise in price. Yet the prices of automobiles failed to rise when Ford shut down despite its having been the dominant producer. Other manufacturers increased their output, and prices *fell* by mid-1927

[12]Paul McCracken and Thomas Moore, Statement to the Subcommittee on Antitrust and Monopoly, U.S. Senate, March 29, 1973; reprinted as *Competition and Market Concentration in the American Economy* (Washington, D.C.: American Enterprise Institute, 1974).

[13]John McGee, *In Defense of Industrial Concentration* (New York: Praeger Publishers, 1971), p. 77; Sam Peltzman, "The Gains and Losses from Industrial Concentration," *Journal of Law and Economics* 20 (October 1977): 229–63.

[14]Dean Worcester, *Bigness, Monopoly and Welfare* (Seattle: University of Washington Press, 1967), pp. 3, 83. Woodrow Wilson, the signer of the Clayton and Federal Trade Commission Acts, stated in his *The New Freedom* (New York and Garden City: Doubleday, Page & Company, 1913), p. 166: "... any large corporation built up by the legitimate processes of business, by economy, by efficiency, is natural; and I am not afraid of it, no matter how big it grows. It can stay big only by doing its work more efficiently than anybody else."

despite the complete withdrawal of the Ford supply of newly manufactured cars from the market.[15]

The fact that a dominant producer has, at most, a very short-lived ability to influence the price of a product can be illustrated by numerous anecdotes. The American Sugar Refining Company merged 98 percent of the capacity for refining sugar east of the Rockies in 1891 and 1892. By cutting production, it managed to raise refining margins by 40 percent in 1893 (which raised the price of sugar by 8 percent). Expansion of output in other firms cut sugar refining margins in 1894 to a level little higher than the 1891 margins despite further reductions in output by American Sugar. By 1894, the entry of additional capacity had forced margins back nearly to 1891 levels and had cut American's share of the sugar business by one-quarter. American was still a dominant firm by today's FTC definition, but it had lost all influence over price and output despite its 85 percent share of capacity.[16]

In 1901, American Can merged 90 percent of all capacity in the can business. It raised prices by one-quarter and lost one-third of its share of market in short order despite additional buying up of competitors and their output. Prices returned to the premerger level in a very short time.

These are the most successful monopolizing cases I can find aside from the Airline Pilots Association, the Teamsters, and similar labor unions.[17] What they demonstrate is that a dominant firm quickly ceases to have any influence in the market if it

[15]Federal Trade Commission, *Report on Motor Vehicle Industry* (Washington, D.C.: U.S. Government Printing Office, 1939), p. 634.

[16]Richard Zerbe, "The American Sugar Refinery Company, 1887–1914: The Story of Monopoly," *Journal of Law and Economics* 12 (October 1969): 353–57.

[17]Y. Brozen, "The Consequences of Economic Regulation," *New Guard* 15 (June 1975): 12–15. Richard Posner, "Exclusionary Practices and the Antitrust Laws," *University of Chicago Law Review* 41 (Spring 1974): 507, states that "U.S. Steel apparently had such a large fraction of the productive capacity of the steel industry that it could obtain monopoly profits by limiting its output." However, the data on capacity and output appear to indicate the opposite to be the case. In 1901 and 1902, with 44 percent of U.S. ingot capacity, U.S. Steel produced 65 percent of ingot output. In 1903 and 1904, as demand for steel fell during the recession, U.S. Steel cut output but other firms increased their production. Only when U.S. Steel *conspired* with other firms during the 1907–1908 recession and all acted in concert did any monopoly influence appear in the steel market. The profitability data for U.S. Steel also appears to contradict Posner. Arthur S. Dewing, "A Statistical Test of Consolidations," *Quarterly Journal of Economics* 36 (November 1921): 84–101, found profits of the separate companies merged to form U.S. Steel were greater than those of U.S. Steel after the merger.

charges a supracompetitive price. In some cases, a dominant firm willing to restrict output greatly has *no* ability to obtain a supracompetitive price even in the short run.

Dominant firms, that is, firms which sell a major part of all products sold, remain dominant only if they charge the competitive price *and* are more efficient than other firms in their industries. If they are less efficient, they soon find their market share dwindling despite selling at competitive prices. The Big Four in the meat packing industry, for example, have seen their share of the market dwindle from 56% in 1935 (and from an even higher share in earlier years) to 47% in 1947 to 38% in 1956 to 22% in 1972.[18] The relative inefficiency of the Big Four showed in the 1920s when their rates of return on investment ran at one-third the rate earned by smaller companies.[19] That situation continued up to at least 1972, and market share of these inefficient firms fell.

The Big Four meat packers (the Big Five in the 1917 FTC investigation) originally achieved a large market share in meat packing by their efficiency—by instituting assembly line methods with complete utilization of all by-products. They became known for using "everything but the squeal." Also, their development of refrigerated packing houses, cold storage, the refrigerator car, and an efficient distribution system created enlarged markets for meat supplied from cheaper livestock sources. They grew large by being innovative. Once their innovations were imitated by other packers, the decline of the Big Four began, accelerating with the spread of highways and the rise of trucking.

The "dominance" of the Big Four did not give them any power to restrict output or to control price. If anything, the rise of the Big Four decreased the dominance of local markets by local butchers who had to compete with fresh meat brought in by train by the Big Four,[20] especially after state laws prohibiting the sale of "foreign" meat were ruled unconstitutional. Nevertheless, the

---

[18]The 1956 and subsequent figures overstate the share of market retained by the original Big Four since Cudahy was displaced by Hormel.

[19]Ralph C. Epstein, *Industrial Profits in the United States* (New York: National Bureau of Economic Research, 1934), pp. 43, 373, reports that twenty-three leading meat packers earned 1.9% on equity in 1928 while forty-six minor meat packers earned 10.0%. In 1964, leading packers earned 3.7% while small packers earned 13.6%.

[20]Ambrose Winston, "The Chimera of Monopoly," *The Atlantic Monthly,* November 1924; reprinted in *The Freeman,* September 1960.

FTC filed one of its earliest "shared monopoly" suits in September 1948 against Armour, Cudahy, Swift, and Wilson, accusing them of "conducting...operations...along parallel noncompetitive lines." They had served consumers too well, thus incurring the hostility of local butchers in the late nineteenth century and the first quarter of this century. Long after local packers began outcompeting the Big Four, in the second quarter of the century, the FTC, in a flagrantly anticonsumer action, rode to rescue the fair maidens who by now had grown mustaches and developed larger biceps than the Big Four. The FTC demanded that Armour and Swift each be broken into five companies and that Cudahy and Wilson each be broken into two firms. The FTC reluctantly dropped the suit in March 1954, nearly six years and millions of dollars in legal costs after it was brought, but only because the court ruled that pre-1930 behavior was irrelevant in a 1950s proceeding.

Why Are Dominant Firms Being Attacked?

The attacks on concentration, whether in the form of an attack on a "dominant" firm or a "shared monopoly," seem to be fairly episodic. The question to be asked is why large firms with a large share of the market are left undisturbed for long periods and then turned on at other times. It is not purely coincidental that the nation suffered deflation from 1882 to 1890, prices dropping by 25 percent in that interval, and the Sherman Act was passed in 1890. At that time, the declining prices were blamed on "cut-throat" and "predatory" competition—and this was also a period in which economies of scale in manufacturing, combined with a rapidly declining cost of transportation, led to centralization of production in enlarged facilities.

From 1867 to 1877, for example, sugar production doubled, from one-half to one million tons annually, and the number of refineries decreased from 60 to 27. In the same period, railroad freight rates fell by 60 percent.[21] The economies of centralized production, together with reduced transport costs, led to larger plants supplying more distant markets at lower prices than the smaller plants resident in those markets. So the myth of "cut-throat" competition and "predatory" pricing was born in this

21The average rail rate fell from 19 mills per ton-mile to 7.5 mills.

and many other industries. Antitrust cases were brought against dominant firms such as American Sugar, Standard Oil, American Tobacco, etc.

Another deflation in which prices again dropped by 25 percent, from 1929 to 1933, again led to animus against "Big Business" and especially against that rising innovation in marketing, the chain store.[22] The investigations of the Temporary National Economic Committee once again directed the country's ire toward dominant firms and industrial concentration. Antitrust cases were brought against dominant firms such as Alcoa and A & P and against "shared monopolies" as in the Mother Hubbard case against the petroleum companies, the proceeding against the major cigarette companies, and the FTC case against the Big Four in meat packing.

Currently, we are trying to find scapegoats for inflation.[23] So we have brought cases against "dominant" firms such as IBM, AT&T, and Du Pont, and against the "shared monopolies" already described.

When we are troubled by deflation or by inflation, both brought on by the government's ineptness in operating our monetary and fiscal policy, the politicians export the blame to somebody else. Mr. Carter tells us in his speeches that the government is not at fault for our inflation—it is up to business and labor to bring inflation to a halt.

In this modern day, we are no longer subject to the kind of superstitions that led the early colonists to hang witches when they were troubled by forces they did not understand. Instead, in this enlightened age, when we seek to rid ourselves of inflation and other mysterious ailments, we pillory dominant firms or the Big Fours in concentrated, and not so concentrated, industries.

The Potential Losses from Deconcentration

This absurd behavior by our politicians and its acceptance by the electorate as being something more than a hunt by politicians for

---

[22]Y. Brozen, "Foreword" to Richard Posner, *The Robinson-Patman Act: Federal Regulation of Price Differences* (Washington, D.C.: American Enterprise Institute, 1976), pp. iii–viii.

[23]J. Cotlin, "Increased Corporation Antitrust Suits Prompt Industry Fears of New Federal Policy," *National Journal Reports,* Sept. 15, 1973, p. 1371.

witches to blame for their own mistakes might be tolerable if it were nothing more than expensive entertainment of voters. But it is something more. It is counterproductive in terms of the ends we seek—less inflation, higher rates of growth, and improved levels of living.

Prices have gone up less rapidly in our most concentrated industries than in others, and productivity has grown more rapidly. From 1967 to 1973, prices for our most concentrated industries rose less than half as rapidly as prices in all manufacturing.[24] From 1958 to 1965, prices in our most concentrated manufacturing industries actually fell while prices in other manufacturing industries rose. Yet it is our concentrated industries with a superior record for moderating inflation and a superb record for increasing productivity that are being cast in the role of economic villains.[25]

If this witch-hunt continues, the result will be economic disaster. If we deconcentrate all our manufacturing industries in which four firms produce more than 50 percent of the product, the result will be a 20 percent rise in costs and a 10 to 15 percent rise in prices.[26] If we want to hasten our decline to the status of a banana republic, the attack on concentration will contribute to that end.

[24]Steven Lustgarten, *Industrial Concentration and Inflation* (Washington, D.C.: American Enterprise Institute, 1975), table 2. P. David Qualls, "Market Structure and Price Behavior in U.S. Manufacturing, 1967–1972," Federal Trade Commission, Bureau of Economics, Working Paper No. 6 (March 1977), also finds a negative relationship between price changes and concentration.

[25]Shirley Scheiba, "Monopoly the Villain," *Barrons,* Nov. 4, 1974, pp. 9, 18–20; "Economic Concentration: The Perennial Fall Guy," *First National Bank Monthly Economic Letter,* April 1972, pp. 12–15.

[26]Sam Peltzman, "The Gains and Losses from Industrial Concentration," *Journal of Law and Economics* 20 (October 1977): 229–263.

RECOMMENDED READING

Armentano, D. T. *The Myths of Antitrust: Economic Theory and Legal Cases.* New Rochelle, N.Y.: Arlington House, 1972.

Benham, Lee. "The Effect of Advertising on the Price of Eyeglasses." *Journal of Law and Economics* 15 (1972): 337–52.

Bork, Robert. *The Antitrust Paradox: A Policy at War with Itself.* New York: Basic Books, 1978.

———. "Vertical Integration and the Sherman Act: The Legal History of an Economic Misconception." *University of Chicago Law Review* 22 (1954–55): 157–201.

Brozen, Yale. "The Impact of FTC Advertising Policies on Competition." In *Advertising and the Public Interest,* edited by S. F. Divita. Chicago: American Marketing Assn., 1974.

———. *The Competitive Economy.* Morristown, N.J.: General Learning Press, 1975.

———. "The Effect of Statutory Minimum Wage Increases on Teen-Age Employment." *Journal of Law and Economics* 12 (April 1969): 109–22.

———, ed. *Advertising and Society.* New York: New York University Press, 1974.

Chandler, Alfred D., Jr. "The Beginnings of 'Big Business' in American Industry." *Business History Review* 33 (Spring 1959): 1–31.

Demsetz, Harold. *The Market Concentration Doctrine: An Examination of Evidence and a Discussion of Policy.* Washington, D.C.: American Enterprise Institute, 1973.

Elzinga, Kenneth G. "Predatory Pricing: The Case of the Gunpowder Trust." *Journal of Law and Economics* 13 (April 1970): 223–40.

Fleming, Harold. *Ten Thousand Commandments: A Story of the Antitrust Laws.* New York: Arno Press, 1972.

Garraty, John A. "The New Deal, National Socialism and the Great Depression." *American Historical Review* 77 (September 1972): 907–44.

Gort, Michael, and Singamseth, Rao. "Concentration and Profit Rates: New Evidence on an Old Issue." *Explorations in Economic Research* 3 (Winter 1976): 1–20.

Hayek, Friedrich A., ed. *Collectivist Economic Planning*. London: Routledge and Kegan Paul, 1935.

Hilton, George. "The Consistency of the Interstate Commerce Act." *Journal of Law and Economics* 9 (October 1966): 87–113.

Kolko, Gabriel. *Railroads and Regulation, 1877–1916*. Princeton, N.J.: Princeton University Press, 1965.

———. *The Triumph of Conservatism: A Reinterpretation of American History 1900–1916*. New York: Free Press, 1977.

Levine, Michael E. "Landing Fees and the Airport Congestion Problem." *Journal of Law and Economics* 12 (April 1969): 79–108.

———. "Is Regulation Necessary? California Air Transportation and National Regulatory Policy." *Yale Law Journal* 74 (July 1965): 1416–47.

Littlechild, Stephen C. *The Fallacy of the Mixed Economy: An "Austrian" Critique of Conventional Economics and Government Policy*. San Francisco: Cato Institute, 1979.

McGee, John S. "Predatory Price Cutting: The Standard Oil (N.J.) Case." *Journal of Law and Economics* 1 (October 1958): 137–69.

———. *In Defense of Industrial Concentration*. New York: Praeger, 1971.

Moore, Thomas G. "The Purpose of Licensing." *Journal of Law and Economics* 4 (October 1961): 93–117.

———. "The Beneficiaries of Trucking Regulation." *Journal of Law and Economics* 21 (October 1978): 327–43.

Nash, Gerald D. "F.D.R. and the World War I Origins of Early New Deal Labor Policy." *Labor History* 1 (Winter 1960): 39–52.

Nutter, G. Warren. *The Extent of Enterprise Monopoly in the United States, 1899–1939: A Quantitative Study of Some Aspects of Monopoly*. Chicago: University of Chicago Press, 1951.

Passer, Harold C. *The Electrical Manufacturers, 1875–1900: A Study in Competition, Entrepreneurship, Technical Change, and Economic Growth*. New York: Arno Press, 1972.

Peltzman, Sam. "An Evaluation of Consumer Protection Legislation: The 1962 Drug Amendments." *Journal of Political Economy* 81 (September-October 1973): 1049–91.

———. "The Effects of Automobile Safety Regulation." *Journal of Political Economy* 83 (August 1975): 677–725.

Posner, Richard A. "A Statistical Study of Antitrust Enforcement." *Journal of Law and Economics* 13 (October 1970): 365–419.

Radosh, Ronald. "The Development of the Corporate Ideology of American Labor Leaders, 1914–1933." Ph.D. dissertation, University of Wisconsin, 1967.

———, and Rothbard, Murray N., eds. *A New History of Leviathan: Essays on the Rise of the American Corporate State.* New York: Dutton, 1972.

Shenoy, Sudha R. "The Sources of Monopoly." *New Individualist Review* 4 (Spring 1966): 41–44.

Stigler, George J. "Public Regulation of the Securities Markets." *Journal of Business* 37 (April 1964): 117–42.

Tyler, Robert L. "The United States Government as Union Organizer: The Loyal Legion of Loggers and Lumbermen." *Mississippi Valley Historical Review* 47 (December 1960): 434–51.

Winston, Ambrose P. *Judicial Economics: The Doctrine of Monopoly as Set Forth by Judges of the U.S. Federal Courts in Suits under the Anti-Trust Laws.* New York: Arno Press, 1972.

Woodridge, William. *Uncle Sam, the Monopoly Man.* New Rochelle, N.Y.: Arlington House, 1971.

Zerbe, Richard. "The American Sugar Refinery Company, 1887–1914: The Story of a Monopoly." *Journal of Law and Economics* 12 (October 1969): 339–75.

ABOUT THE AUTHOR

Yale Brozen is Professor of Business Economics in the Graduate School of Business at the University of Chicago, directs the Program in Applied Economics, and is an Adjunct Scholar, American Enterprise Institute for Public Policy Research.

He has lectured and published in Argentina, Brazil, Peru, Venezuela, Canada, Japan, England, Belgium, Italy, and Switzerland. His professional work has appeared in the *American Economic Review*, the *Journal of Law and Economics*, the *Antitrust Bulletin*, the *Journal of World Trade Law*, the *Antitrust Law Journal, Journal of Business, Political Science Quarterly, American Journal of Economics and Sociology, Barrons,* and numerous other publications. His articles have been translated into French, Italian, Spanish, Portuguese, and Japanese and frequently reprinted in collections and inserted into the *Congressional Record*. Professor Brozen has served as a consultant to major corporations and to various governmental agencies, trade associations, and foundations.

The Cato Papers

1. *Left and Right: The Prospects for Liberty,* by Murray N. Rothbard $2.00

2. *The Fallacy of the Mixed Economy: An "Austrian" Critique of Conventional Economics and Government Policy,* by Stephen C. Littlechild   4.00

3. *Unemployment and Monetary Policy: Government as Generator of the "Business Cycle,"* by Friedrich A. Hayek   2.00

4. *Individualism and the Philosophy of the Social Sciences,* by Murray N. Rothbard   2.00

5. *National Income Statistics: A Critique of Macroeconomic Aggregation,* by Oskar Morgenstern   2.00

6. *A Tiger by the Tail: The Keynesian Legacy of Inflation,* by Friedrich A. Hayek   4.00

7. *Strategic Disengagement and World Peace: Toward a Non-interventionist American Foreign Policy,* by Earl C. Ravenal   2.00

8. *A Theory of Strict Liability: Toward a Reformulation of Tort Law,* by Richard A. Epstein   4.00

9. *Is Government the Source of Monopoly? and Other Essays,* by Yale Brozen   2.00

10. *A Property System Approach to the Electromagnetic Spectrum: A Legal–Economic–Engineering Study,* by Arthur S. De Vany, Ross D. Eckert, Charles J. Meyers, Donald J. O'Hara, and Richard C. Scott   4.00

11. *Fiat Money Inflation in France,* by Andrew Dickson White   4.00

12. *Revisionism: A Key to Peace and Other Essays,* by Harry Elmer Barnes   4.00

13. *The Great Depression and New Deal Monetary Policy: Two Essays,* by Garet Garrett and Murray N. Rothbard   4.00

Reprinted by the Cato Institute, the Papers in this series have been selected for their singular contributions to such fields as economics, history, philosophy, and public policy.

Copies of the *Cato Papers* may be ordered from the Publications Department, Cato Institute, 747 Front Street, San Francisco, California 94111.